Diego Javier Bastidas Logrono

Implementation of the LDAP protocol in the establishment of a domain

Diego Javier Bastidas Logrono

Implementation of the LDAP protocol in the establishment of a domain

Implementation of the LDAP protocol in the establishment of a domain with free software in Linux in the 11 BCB Galapagos

ScienciaScripts

Table of Contents :

DEDICATION

The completion of the thesis represents only the smallest part of all the effort made throughout this time. I dedicate it to God and Jesus Christ first because thanks to their love and blessing none of this was a reality; to my parents Cesar and Monserratt, my daughter Andrea, Sariah, and those to come; to my professor Wladimir Castro Salazar who helped me to strive in the career of systems.

Diego Javier

THANK YOU

My gratitude is to the life that God my loving Father Elohim has given me to be tested in this world, to Jesus Christ who is my Savior, who loves me, to my earthly parents who have always been the best example that a son could have had, to my uncle Wellington Fernando Logroño Calderón, who from the spirit world has supported me in every goal, to my grandparents and beloved relatives, and my teachers who have guided me throughout this career that advances every day.

Diego Javier

EXECUTIVE OVERVIEW

The development of communications in this time has advanced by leaps and bounds, due to this, the development of free software under Linux in companies has been crucial because with the implementation of the Free Directory Access Protocol on Linux servers will help the BRIGADA DE CABALLERÍA BLINDADA No. 11 "GALÁPAGOS" to control unauthorized users to access information that is reserved and confidential.

The unauthorized access to the information would cause instability in the Institution, so this proposal based on the implementation of a Domain with the LDAP protocol and its application in the establishment of a domain with free software under Linux and its application in the BRIGADA DE CABALLERÍA BLINDADA No.11 "GALÁPAGOS" will allow the creation of a reliable authentication domain for both Windows and Linux in addition to providing computer security especially for the Look over the Shoulder attack.

We present for consideration the results of the research whose main purpose is to implement LDAP authentication in the network users of the 11 B.C.B. "GALÁPAGOS" which will provide reliability in computers, to be applied in any public and private institution that wants secure authentication with this protocol.

ABSTRACT

The development of communications at this time has advanced by leaps and bounds because of this, the development of free software under Linux in companies has been crucial since the implementation of the Protocol Free Access to Directories in Linux servers will help the BRIGADA DE CABALLERIA BLINDADA No11 "GALÁPAGOS" to control unauthorized users to access information that is privileged and confidential.

Unauthorized access to information would cause instability in the institution, so this proposal based on the implementation of an LDAP-domain and its application in the establishment of a domain with free software under Linux and its application in BRIGADA DE CABALLERIA BLINDADA No. 11 "GALÁPAGOS" will create an authentication realm reliable for both Windows and Linux in addition to providing information security especially for the attack on the Shoulder Look.

Is presented for consideration the results of research whose main purpose is to implement LDAP authentication in the network users of the 11 BCB GALAPAGOS providing reliability in computers, for application in any public or private institution that wishes to secure authentication protocol.

INTRODUCTION

This work aims to analyze the relevant aspects of the Free Directory Access Protocol, taking as a practical case the Data Network of the BRIGADA DE CABALLERÍA BLINDADA No.11 GALÁPAGOS (by its acronym 11 B.C.B. GALAPÁGOS). The implementation of an optimal Linux platform that allows the incorporation of new services that contribute to increase the level of security in user accounts, passwords, a proxy server, enabling network users to have better features and improve their work. Nowadays, the use of open source in servers has spread to practically all data communication networks, boosted mainly by the expansion of the Internet, as well as corporate and cooperation networks associated with this technology. Network design was based on features such as functionality, but not security, conditions that are cost-effective from a business point of view in the short term, but can be expensive in the long term. In order to analyze and develop the design of a secure network, it is necessary to know the details and characteristics of the underlying communications protocols, which will be responsible for transporting the information and data to be distributed. At the same time, the services provided in the network and their operating details must be analyzed. In the present work we have chosen to give an eminently technical approach, starting by applying basic features of the client-server type protocol to access an existing directory service in the protocols from a practical point of view taking as a case of the data network of the BRIGADA DE CABALLERÍA BLINDADA No.11 "GALÁPAGOS", complemented with a practical vision provided by the existing tools to allow or deny the execution of the mentioned features. The information existing today, both in the traditional bibliography (books, magazines, technical articles.) and on the Internet itself (Web pages, mailing lists, news groups.) regarding the generic topic addressed in this document, "Free Directory Access Protocol", as well as the associated vulnerabilities and protections, is really extensive, and any computer scientist will be able to delve into this exciting world of open source. It should be taken into account that some of the topics covered cannot be analyzed in depth, since the detailed introduction of the concepts that these technologies include would require abundant documentation, and by themselves could constitute a work of similar length to the present one.

The BRIGADE OF ARMORED CABALLERY No.11 GALÁPAGOS as an institution of military character, is a fundamental part of the progress of the country whose motto is "ARMORED CABALLERY, VICTORY AND FREEDOM'S BALUARTS". Its specific functions are: To have the highest level of integrated systematic credibility, with professional, ethical and morally qualified personnel, with capacity to face the new scenarios that guarantee peace, security and that collaborate with the development of the nation, with special attention in the indigenous rural communities, rural and marginal urban areas, to reinforce the civic-military link, to strengthen the civic feeling and pride of our nationality, in order to collaborate in the socio-economic development of the country.

The "BRIGADA DE CABALLERÍA BLINDADA No. 11 GALÁPAGOS" is an organizational structure where Internet technology is widely accepted. However, in our province and in particular in the "BRIGADA DE CABALLERÍA BLINDADA No.11 GALÁPAGOS" few formal investigations are carried out in aspects related to LDAP servers, and in a public institution this is a critical success factor for its security in user authentication.

The "BRIGADA DE CABALLERÍA BLINDADA No. 11 GALÁPAGOS", has a data network, with a server room and access points to it in each of the Departments and Units. At present, it provides the following services to the respective users.

- A network domain.
- Internet service.

It does not have other additional services such as ldap server, mail server, reliable firewall, etc. Information has always been an invaluable asset and protecting it has been an ongoing and vitally important task. As new techniques for protecting information are created, curious people devise ways to gain unauthorized access to it. Computer networks are no exception. Security is not just an implementation of new software capable of protecting information, but rather a change in thinking and careful action. If the LDAP protocol is not implemented, the BRIGADA DE CABALLERÍA BLINDADA No.11 GALÁPAGOS will be subject to constant computer security attacks and any person could access your computer without any permission and become a victim of a computer fraud especially the computer attack of Look over the Shoulder, with the possibility of happening a great fraud that would be playing with the National Defense Security.

This work is particularly directed to the "BRIGADA DE CABALLERÍA BLINDADA No. 11 GALÁPAGOS de la ciudad de Riobamba", because some aspects within the intranets are specific to each institution, such as technological infrastructure, organizational structure, etc. The beneficiaries are all users with access to a computer on the network. This project has as fundamental importance to perform an analysis and implementation of the LDAP protocol in the institution's server and, given the impossibility of reviewing each and every one of the existing problems, it has been chosen to select a significant set close to the needs of the institution. According to the research carried out, there is no service equal or similar to the one proposed that allows the availability of network services, nor any security policy that allows access to the directory information by means of a schema:

-1-Client-server.
-2-Define a hierarchical structure of objects or entries in the form of a tree.
-3-Interactivity with the user, authentication.

In addition, it is necessary to avoid any type of computer attack, in a more secure and reliable way. The implementation of these services will be a success factor to achieve the objectives proposed by the institution.

The following general objective is proposed: "To implement the LDAP protocol and its establishment in a domain with free software under Linux in the BRIGADA DE CABALLERÍA BLINDADA No.11 "GALÁPAGOS" (Armored Cavalry Brigade No.11 "GALÁPAGOS").
Once the general objective has been analyzed and in order to comply with it, the following Specific Objectives are proposed:
 -1- Preliminary Study of the LDAP protocol
 -2- Identify the characteristics of the LDAP Protocol within the virtual environment of
Open Source under Linux.
 -3- Adopt a design guide of a Domain in the LDAP Protocol in Linux.
 -4- Implement the free directory access protocol.

CHAPTER I

1. METHODOLOGICAL FRAMEWORK

This chapter presents the methodology used to develop the LDAP protocol project. Aspects such as the type of research, techniques and procedures that were used to carry out the project are discussed.

1.1. TYPE OF RESEARCH

This project can be catalogued in its first instance as an **exploratory** type of research since the following will be carried out:

-1-   **A problem is formulated:** Difficulty in finding information about applications developed in technology and platforms little used in the country on the implementation of the free protocol of access to directories with free software.

-2-   **Information on the subject is gathered:** information will be compiled from various bibliographic and electronic sources to make a detailed study of the subject.

-3-   **Concepts are clarified:** it is very important to be clear about many concepts of the Linux technology to be applied before starting to experiment with it.

Once the exploratory part has concluded, the research will be categorized as **experimental for the** following reasons:

-4-   **A phenomenon will be provoked in order to test something: once the** Open LDAP technology is mastered, it will be systematized, using Open Source, and the respective modifications, improvements and implementation will be established.

-5-   **A logical and systematic approach to scientific experimentation is required:** the improvement of academic research will be demonstrated by experimenting with the various technologies and platforms that Open LDAP provides for implementing secure user accounts for directory access.

1.2. SOURCES OF INFORMATION

They have been classified into two:

-1- Primary Sources

-2- Secondary Sources

1.2.1. PRIMARY SOURCES

It is necessary to use the following information gathering techniques:

Observation: This technique together with the experience gained in previous pre-professional practices will be an important source of information.

Surveys: The present research work will be tested through the study that will try to solve most of the problems of the research that through the survey will obtain information of the thoughts and criteria of the surveyed personnel through the use of questionnaires designed in a clear way for obtaining specific information.

1.2.2. SECONDARY SOURCES

For the development of the present work, sufficient written and electronic information on the subject will be compiled, which can be classified into the following categories:

-1-   Books: books in digital format LDAP, and other software development technologies in virtual environments, Linux manuals.

-2-   E-books: will provide the most updated information about Open Source.

-3-   Magazines, articles and technical documents: information related to Open ldap, Linux (Suse Operating System) and real application cases of this with our current computer network technology.

-4-   On-screen documentation: aids and documentation mainly on the development packages and kits that are used for the execution of the thesis.

1.3. RESEARCH METHODS

The methods to be used in this research are as follows:

1.3.1. EXPLORATORY RESEARCH METHOD

We will gather as much information about the implementation of the LDAP protocol with Open Source as possible, and postpone the task of removing unnecessary data until we get a workable application for servers and clients as demonstrated here with Suse Linux.

1.3.2. EXPERIMENTAL SCIENTIFIC RESEARCH METHOD

This method will allow testing the feasible project on the basis of practical case studies (experiments), the results will be analyzed and disseminated and applied as a feasible project in the BRIGADA DE CABALLERIA BLINDADA No.11 "GALÁPAGOS" (Armored Cavalry Brigade No.11 "GALÁPAGOS").

This method performs the following steps:

-1-   **Observation:** The different Linux systems applied to LDAP servers will be observed in order to mount the optimal operating system on the server that meets the requirements of the institution.

-2-   **Experimentation:** We will test the different Linux distributions in operating systems such as Centos, Ubuntu, Fedora, Red Hat, Suse and we will choose the option that works in a simpler way with the LDAP protocol.

-3-   **Comparison:** The Linux distributions will be compared and we will choose the most reliable, secure and fast to implement which is Suse Linux with the gq and yast application.

-4-   **Generalization:** This implementation of the LDAP protocol, tested on the main server of the 11BCB "GALÁPAGOS" and on virtual machines, will be applied.

1.4. POPULATION

All personnel with access to a computer within the Internal Network of the BRIGADA DE CABALLERÍA BLINDADA No.11 "GALÁPAGOS", which is a total of sixty-seven (67) users.

1.5. SAMPLE

The time required to analyze all interactions of military personnel with the LDAP protocol will depend on the surveys conducted and their results. Only development technologies that have been applied to develop applications at UNIDEC (Linux, ipv4, ipv6, etc.) will be considered. Then, the sample is delimited in the following way making the corresponding calculation for the Observation by means of Surveys, for the IMPLEMENTATION OF THE LDAP PROTOCOL IN THE ESTABLISHMENT OF A DOMAIN WITH FREE SOFTWARE UNDER LINUX IN THE BRIGADE OF ARMORED CABALLERY No.11 "GALÁPAGOS" reliable for Windows and Linux.

$1 - a = 95\%$

$Z = 1,96$

$E = 3\%$

$E = 0,03$

$P = 0,5$

$P + q = 1$

$Q = 1 - p$

$Q = 1 - 0,5$

$Q = 0,5$

Then:

N=67 Users

Z=1,96

E=0.03

P=0,5

Q=0,5

No= Z 0 . P . Q / EE

No=(1.96) 0 . 0.5.0.5 / 0.030

No= 3.84 . 0.25 / 0.0009

No=0.96 / 0.0009

No=1067

Then:

N = No / 1 + (No-1)/N

N'=**1067** /1   + (1067 - 1) /67

N = 63

This means that the survey will be applied to 63 users.

CHAPTER II

2 . THEORETICAL FRAMEWORK

1.1. FRAME OF REFERENCE

1.1.1. PLACE OF DEVELOPMENT

According to Command Order No.11 004-III-C-974 of March 27, 1974, the creation of the ARMY BRIGADE No.11 "GALÁPAGOS" was ordered, with headquarters in SAN PEDRO DE RIOBAMBA, based on Decree No.11246 of February 18, 1974, after the approval of the organic regulations of the army. of February 18, 1974, after the approval of the organic regulation of the army, it is so, between the months of August and October 1974, the unit was transferred to the camp "San Nicolas" in the city of Riobamba, being its first Commander Mr. Crnl. Américo Álava, and of the Armored Reconnaissance Squadron, Lieutenant Colonel René Silva, with the cooperation of the troops and the initiative of the officers playing an important role. Since then, loyalty, comradeship, esprit de corps, are feelings present in the Armored Cavalry soldier and constitute the fundamental pillars on which the armed institution is based, that with effort, sacrifice and self-improvement, strive to achieve the goal of being an excellent military professional, leader and conductor. On the twenty-ninth day of August 1985, according to Command Order No.11 011-985, the General Command of the Army, ordered the merger of the Cavalry and Armored Forces, under the name "Armored Cavalry". In April 1989, according to ministerial resolution No.11 027, in its article 7°, authorizes the integrated merger of the current Cavalry and Armored Forces of the Army, with this last definitive disposition, based on the one already issued in 1985, and in consideration, to the organic for the years 1987-1992, in which a new organization of the tank platoons is considered, and before the initiative and interest of the Command of the 11-BCB "GALÁPAGOS", the idea of materializing the groups of Armored Cavalry is reborn. With this concept, the military institution forges conductors capable of facing technological development and new challenges, using their knowledge to strengthen institutional development, achieving the best professional performance in their functions. The deed of April 21, 1822, immortal glory of our heroes, was enlivened and renewed by the spirit of national solidarity and the combative impetus of our soldiers, who reedited the Tapi campaign and covered themselves with honor and glory in a masterful battle for the dignity, sovereignty and rights of the homeland.

We must never forget our ancestors, true innate and perhaps forgotten heroes; that we must never underestimate the best of our lives, which is honor and dignity.

2.1 .2. ARCHITECTURE

Units of the ARMORED CABALLERY BRIGADE No.11 "GALÁPAGOS".

-I-Command   and General Staff.

    -I-Group of Armored Cavalry   No.31 "MACHALA".

    -I-Group of Armored Cavalry   No.32 "AZUAY".

    -I Armored Cavalry Group   No. 33 "TAPI" -I   Armored Cavalry Group   No. 33
"TAPI" -I Armored Cavalry Group No. 33 "TAPI".

    -I-Armored Cavalry School   of the "F-T".

    -I-Self-Propelled Artillery Group   No. 11 TNTE. RODRIGUEZ".

    -I-Aircraft Antiaircraft Artillery Group No.12 "CAPE QUIROZ".

    -I-Reconnaissance and Security Squadron   . No.11. "EPICLACHIMA".

    -I-Logistic Support Command No.11 "CALICUCHIMA"   -I-Logistic Support Command
No.11 "CALICUCHIMA".

    -I-Communications Squadron No.11 "RUMIÑAHUI".

    I-Armored Engineer Squadron No.11 "CENEPA"   -I-Armored Engineer Squadron No.11
"CENEPA"   -I-Armored Engineer Squadron No.11 "CENEPA".

    -I-Military Police Squadron   No.11

-I-Peloton   Band of Musicians No. 11

    -I-Civic Support and Forestry Squadron No.11

-I-Hospital   de BRIGADA No.11 "GALÁPAGOS" -I-Hospital de BRIGADA No.11
"GALÁPAGOS".

2.1.   THEORETICAL FOUNDATION

2.1.1.   FREE DIRECTORY ACCESS PROTOCOL

LDAP (Free Directory Access Protocol) is an application-level protocol that allows access to an
ordered and distributed directory service to search for various information in a network environment.
It is also considered as a database (although its storage system may be different) to which queries can
be made. Typically, it stores login or access information to a system (username and password) and is
used for authentication, although it is possible to store other information (user contact details, location
of various network resources, permissions, certificates, etc.).

In conclusion, LDAP is a protocol for unified access to a set of information on a network. There are
several implementations and real applications of the LDAP protocol. The great diversity of

information that can be stored in these directories makes it suitable for use in applications such as:

-1-   White or yellow pages directories

-2-   E-mail servers

-3-   Domain Name Servers (DNS)

-4-   Repositories for digital certificates

-5-   User account repositories

The free directory access protocol is a message-oriented client/server protocol.

This means that a client program, running on some computer, constructs a message requesting a certain action and sends it over the network to another computer running a server program. This server program receives the request, performs some action and returns some result to the client.

Figure.N°1 Relationship between client and LDAP server

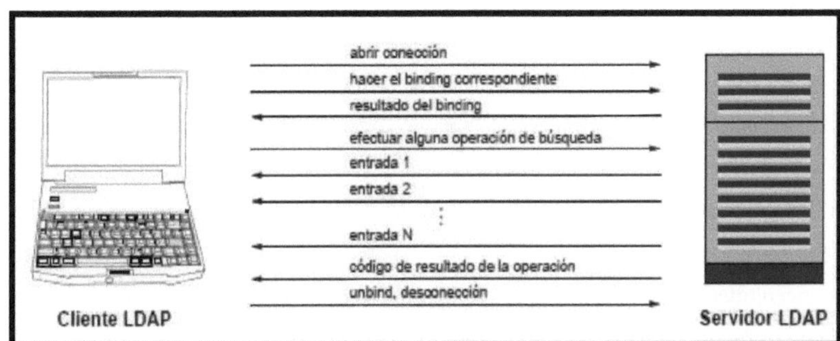

Source: Howes T., "The String Representation of LDAP Search Filters", RFC 2254,December 1997.

1.1.1.1. REPLICAS

An LDAP server can, either for security or performance reasons, have copies of itself in other LDAP servers, of course, always respecting a Master-Slave hierarchy, thus greatly reducing the bottlenecks that could be generated if there is only one LDAP server to handle all requests. It should be noted that only the master server will be able to make modifications to the directory, i.e. the slave servers can only perform query operations on the information contained in them. If at any time a user requests a modification operation on a slave directory, it will send a request to the master server to carry out such modification, and once the modification has been made, the master server will update the information contained in all the slave directories under its responsibility. The basis for the popularity of the LDAP protocol lies in its simplicity of implementation and use, as well as the speed of access to information compared to a database.

Figure.N°2 LDAP replication

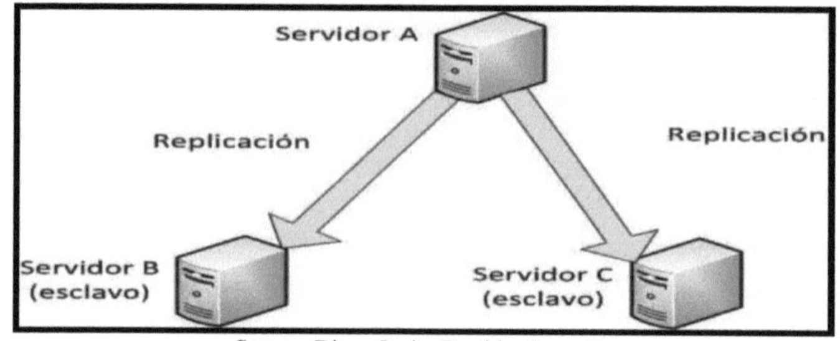

Source: Diego Javier Bastidas Logroño

1.1.1.2. REFERENCES TO OTHER LDAP DIRECTORIES

A referral is a link that connects two LDAP servers and is used to point to the server that should continue a search when the referring server is unable to satisfy a request. There are two types of referrals: referrals to superior knowledge servers and referrals to subordinate servers. A referral to a higher knowledge server is made when a directory, which is contained in a higher hierarchy directory, did not produce any search results, then, since the higher hierarchy directory is likely to be able to satisfy the query request, the search request is sent to it in the form of a referral. When a directory is configured in a distributed manner, it is necessary to organize the information contained in each of the LDAP servers in such a way that a hierarchy is respected, the way to do this is by means of references that go from the servers of higher hierarchy to those of lower hierarchy. With this it will be possible to have control over all the information and at the same time a better performance since not being concentrated all the information in a single server the workload is distributed among all the servers that conform the directory.

Figure.N°3 References between two LDAP servers

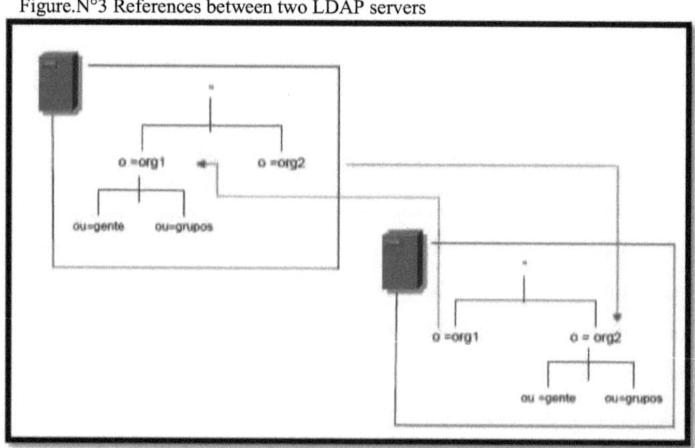

Source: Howes T., and M. Smith, "The LDAP URL Format," RFC 2255, December 1997.

1.1.1.3. LDAP HISTORY

In the 1970s two communication standards were developed separately, OSI and TCP/IP. The OSI model consisted of seven well-defined layers and its development (which did not involve the implementation of applications) was in the hands of a formal committee, namely the CCITT (Consultative Committee on International Telephony and Telegraphy) in conjunction with the ISO (International Standards Organization). TCP/IP, on the other hand, was developed in a much less formal manner where any expert proposed standards through so-called RFCs (Request For Comments) and implementations were left to anyone who wanted to implement a given RFC. In addition, the seven strict layers defined in the OSI model made it a more computational resource-consuming software implementation than TCP/IP, which was not as rigid in its definition of layers. This fact meant that the OSI model could not be implemented on some computers (desktop or personal computers, for example) at that time. Thus, OSI was left with its seven layers defining protocols and applications, which today serve practically only as a reference, since their development was very slow compared to that of TCP/IP. The latter eventually became the standard for Internet communications. Despite this, OSI defined some very important standards that served to inspire TCP/IP similes.

One of these protocols was the X.500 directory service, developed in 1988, which proposes an organization of directory entries in a hierarchically ordered namespace. X.500 also defines powerful search capabilities to make the retrieval of information from directories easier and more optimal. For the interaction between a client and the directory server, the X.500 standard defined the Directory Access Protocol (DAP). However, in order for DAP to operate, OSI layers were required. This fact led to the development of a less resource-intensive directory access protocol that would use TCP/IP instead of the OSI model. This new protocol was initially defined in RFC 1487, "X.500 Lightweight Access Protocol", which was later replaced by RFC 1777, "Free Directory Access Protocol". The latest version of LDAP was proposed in RFC 2251.

LDAP was initially defined as a protocol for accessing an X.500 directory server via TCP/IP since X.500 servers support the DAP protocol for accessing their directories. Thus the LDAP server served as an intermediary between a client that could not implement DAP since it did not have OSI but TCP/IP in its protocols.

Currently the LDAP protocol is implemented with free software under Linux in several cases since it omits the use of paid software with Microsoft providing improvements in speed, greater data flow and network security.

Figure. N° 4 LDAP as TCP/IP intermediary X500 Servers

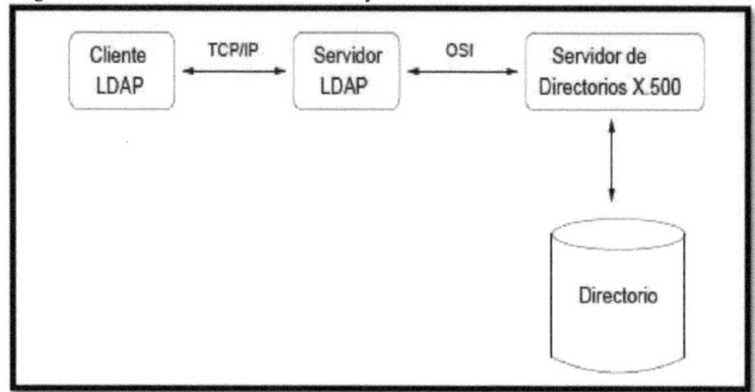

Source: Howes T., "The String Representation of LDAP Search Filters", RFC 2254,December 1997.

However, as already mentioned, TCP/IP grew, and more and more LDAP clients (users in directories, browsers, etc.) were emerging. More LDAP client applications were developed than client applications for X.500 directories.

Given this development, the need for the X.500 directory server was disappearing, and it was thought that the LDAP server would rather access the directories directly. RFC 1777 proposes direct access to X.500 directories. The LDAP protocol using TCP-IP has broadened the vision of the computer scientist to develop and investigate the vast world of free software and the different new protocols that are appearing day by day with a constant practice of research.

An LDAP server that can directly access directories is called a stand-alone LDAP server as shown in the following figure:

Figure. N° 5. Standalone LDAP server

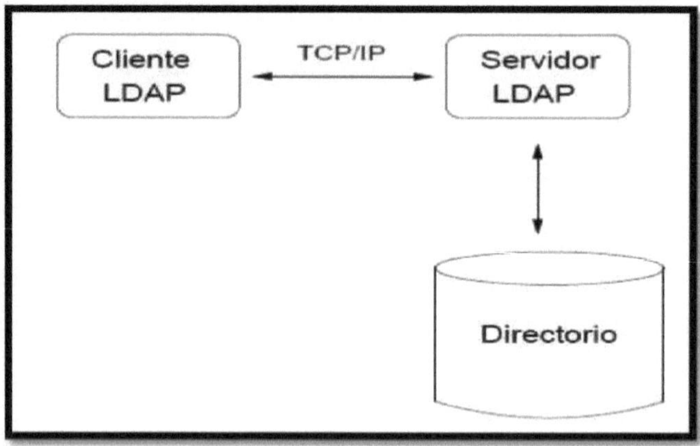

Source: Yeong W.,Howes T., and Kille S., "X.500 Free Directory Access Protocol",RFC 1487, July 1993.

The original version was developed by the University of Michigan. The first version was not used and it was in 1995 that the RFCs (Request For Comments) for LDAP version 2 were published. The RFCs for LDAP version 3 were published in 1997. Version 3 included features such as control access lists and directory replication.

1.1.1.4. ADVANTAGES OF LDAP USER ACCOUNTS

The advantages of maintaining user accounts on an LDAP server are:

Flexibility. It is possible to add attributes to an LDAP account by adding schemas to the entries that make up the accounts. Accounts in Unix for example have a fixed structure and it is not possible to add other fields. The same happens with accounts in other systems such as WindowsNT, however with Linux in the LDAP protocol, attributes such as the user's digital photograph, his digital cryptographic certificate, etc. can be added to the user's data. If in the future an application is created that needs another attribute for each user then that attribute can be added seamlessly to the user's account (entry) in the LDAP directory.

-1-   **Accessibility.** Currently there are some little known applications, both for Linux and Windows, that support user authentication from an LDAP server.

-2-   **Centralization.** This is a consequence of the previous point. Since it is possible to maintain user accounts on an LDAP server and these can be accessed from different operating systems, it is not necessary for each system to manage its own accounts, but instead use an LDAP account server.

1.1.1.5. LDAP INFORMATION MODEL

The LDAP information model defines the types of data and basic units of information that can be stored in a directory. The basic unit of information in a directory is the entry, which is a set of data about an object, such as a person or an organization.

Figure N°6. LDAP structure

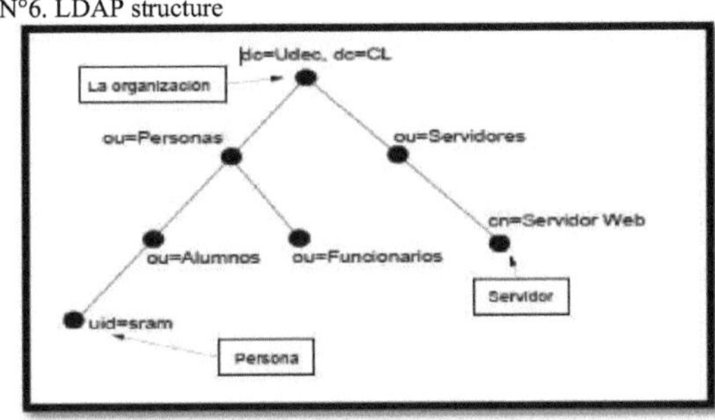

Source: Howes T., and Smith M., "The LDAP Application Program Interface," RFC 1823, August 1995.

Each node corresponds to an entry in the directory.

The LDAP naming model is important because it allows a unique name to be given to each entry in a directory. This unique name in LDAP is called a distinguished name or simply DN, which is constructed from a series of relative distinguished names (RDN) of the particular object, up the tree.

1.1.1.6. LDAP FUNCTIONAL MODEL

The LDAP functional model describes how to access data in the directory through operations that can be performed using the LDAP protocol. The operations of the LDAP functional model are divided into three groups:

-1-   Query operations, which allow searching the directory and retrieving data from it.

-2-   Update operations, which allow you to add, delete, rename or change entries in a directory.

-3-   Authentication and control operations, which allow clients to be identified to the directory server and therefore control certain aspects of the session, such as restricting or allowing access to certain entries.

1.1.1.7. LDAP SECURITY MODEL

The purpose of the LDAP security model is to protect the information in a directory against unauthorized access. The authentication of an LDAP client on a server is part of the security of a directory, so the model seen above, the authentication model, is part of it. Another part of the LDAP security model are the access controls, which are the way in which the privileges that certain users have, after being successfully authenticated, are specified. These access controls to a directory have not yet been standardized, although work is in progress, it is clear that the basic types of privileges to be assigned to clients over certain DNs in a directory are write and/or read. Typically the owner of a given entry in a directory may have write privileges to that entry, while others may only have read privileges to their public data and no privileges to the sensitive data of the user in question. When a client binds to a directory to read public data from an entry, it does not need to provide a key (since the data is public). In this case we speak of anonymous binding. Finally, as mentioned in the previous section, it is possible to encrypt an entire session between a client and an LDAP server using SSL/TLS. This is useful, first at the time of authentication and then for the transfer of sensitive data between the client and the LDAP server.

2.2.2. ACTIVE DIRECTORY

It contains several important features that facilitate its administration similar to LDAP, these features are detailed below:

Scalability: your directory services operate in a small environment, just as in a large distributed network, can grow with any organization and can support a virtually unlimited number of objects.

Extensibility: Administrators can customize the keys and objects that appear within Active Directory to meet the needs of any organization.

Security: access control can be enabled on each object and even on each property of that object, this design allows you to completely control who can have access.

Active Directory supports LDAP, this protocol allows you to easily find objects within Active Directory, which is the name used by Microsoft (since Windows 2000) as a centralized information store for one of its administration domains. Under

this name is actually a schema (definition of the fields that can be queried).

2.2.2.1. ACTIVE DIRECTORY ORGANIZATION

It allows designing a directory structure with easy search criteria so that users can access the resources they need without having to know the physical layout of the network and the location of the different servers, it is organized in a tree structure that contains the resources in a logical way. This organization is explained below:

Domain: The organizational structure is based on the domain, which follows the structure of the network domain, and each domain only stores information about its objects, for practical reasons. Each domain can contain an unlimited number of resources with a theoretical limit of approximately ten million, the domain also acts as a security line so that access rights to resources within the domain can be controlled.

Organizational Units: Domain resources are organized into *Organizational Units* (OU). Imagine an OU as a file folder containing suitable files.

Objects: an object can be any resource in the domain such as files, applications or even users.

Tree: is a grouping of one or more domains, although it is composed of several it is still a unit in the sense that it shares a contiguous namespace, this means that the secondary domain name falls within the DNS naming scheme. For example, the primary domain may be called xyz-company.com, while the secondary domain is called acct.xyz-company.com. All domains within the tree also share the same global catalog, i.e., a listing of objects within that domain.

Forest: is a logical grouping of trees.

Active Directory uses a global catalog that allows users to search for information in a domain, tree, or forest. The global catalog is automatically generated in each domain through the replication process. The Active Directory schema is a list of definitions that determines the objects and information about them that can be stored in Active Directory, which defines these objects through classes, class properties, and attributes. For each class of objects, the schema defines the attributes that these objects must have to be included in a particular class, for example a type of computers will have certain attributes that the objects must meet to be part of that class. These attributes are included in a predetermined form, but they can be tweaked and changed. For each object of a class there are certain well-defined attributes. As an example, a user of the same class users will contain attributes such as: first name, last name, user name, e-mail address, etc. Thanks to these attributes users can have access to the global catalog to search for a particular resource with attributes only.

2.2.3. DIRECTORIES

A directory itself is a database, however, it contains more descriptive and attribute-based information. The information contained in a directory is usually read much more than it is written. As a result, directories do not normally implement the complicated transaction schemas or rollback schemas that databases use to perform complex updates to large volumes of data. Updates to a directory are usually simple all-or-nothing changes, if they allow anything at all. Directories are there to provide fast response to search or query operations. They can have the ability to replicate information widely, in order to increase availability and reliability, while reducing response time. When information in a directory is replicated, temporary inconsistencies between the information in the replicas can be accepted, as long as there is eventually synchronization. There are many ways to provide a directory service. The different methods allow different types of information to be stored in the directory, different requirements for referencing, querying and updating information, the way in which the directory is protected from unauthorized access. Some directory services are local, providing services to a restricted context. Other services are global, providing service in a much broader context.

2.2.4. DIFFERENCE BETWEEN LDAP AND DATABASE

A Database Management System (DBMS) from Sybase, Oracle, Informix or Microsoft is used to process queries or updates to a relational database. These databases can receive hundreds of insert, modify or delete requests per second. An LDAP server is used to process queries to an LDAP directory. But the LDAP protocol processes delete and update requests very slowly. In other words, LDAP is a type of database, but it is not a relational database. It is not designed to process hundreds or thousands of changes per minute like relational systems, but to perform data reads very efficiently. LDAP features include:

-1-   **Relatively static data**: Data stored in directories is not usually updated very frequently.

-2-   **Fast read operations:** Due to the nature of the data stored in the directories, reads are more common than writes.

-3-   **Distributed environment:** easy replication.

-4-   **Hierarchical structure**: Directories natively store information in a hierarchical manner.

-5-   **Object-oriented:** The directory represents elements and objects. Objects are created as entries, which represent a collection of attributes.

-6-   **Standard Scheme:** The directories use a standard system that can be easily used by various applications.

-7-   **Multi-value attributes:** Attributes can store a single value or several values.

-8-   **Multi-master replication:** Many LDAP servers allow writes or updates to be performed on multiple servers.

2.2.5. LDAP OPERATION

It is similar to Active Directory but on Linux. The LDAP directory service is based on a client-server model. One or more LDAP servers contain the data that make up the LDAP directory tree or backbone database, the LDAP client connects to the LDAP server and makes a query. The server responds with a corresponding answer or a hint as to where the client can find more information. No matter which LDAP server the client connects to, it will always see the same directory view; the name presented to one LDAP server refers to the same entry that would be referenced on another LDAP server. Its operation is based on:

-1-   Speed in the reading of records.

-2-   It allows to replicate the server in a very simple and economical way.

-3-   Applications of all types, have LDAP connection interfaces and can be integrated with easily.

-4-   It has a global naming model that ensures that all entries are unique.

-5-   It uses a hierarchical information storage system.

-6-   Allows multiple independent directories.

-7-   It works over TCP/IP and SSL/TLS.

-8-   Most applications have LDAP support.

-9-   Most LDAP servers are easy to install, maintain and optimize.

Open ldap is a free implementation of the protocol that supports multiple schemas so it can be used to connect to any other LDAP. It has its own license, the Open LDAP Public License. Being a platform-independent protocol, several Linux and BSD distributions include it.

Open LDAP has four main components:

-10-   slapd - standalone LDAP daemon.
-11-   slurpd - standalone LDAP update replication daemon.
-12-   LDAP protocol support library routines.
-13-   Utilities, tools and customers.

2.2.6. TICKETS

The LDAP information model is based on entries. An entry is a collection of attributes that have a unique, global Distinguished Name (DN). The DN is unique among all other objects and contains enough information for a user to retrieve the object from the directory, it contains the name of both the domain and the path to that particular object. The DN contains several attributes such as *Domain Component Name* (DC), *Organizational Unit Name* (OU), and a *Common Name* (CN). Each attribute of an entry has a type and one or more values. The types are usually mnemonic words, such as "cn" for common name, or "mail" for a mail address. The syntax of attributes depends on the type of attribute. For example, a cn attribute may contain the value "José Manuel Suárez". An email attribute may contain a value "jmsuarez@ejemplo.com".

Figure N° 7. Inputs - LDAP Attributes

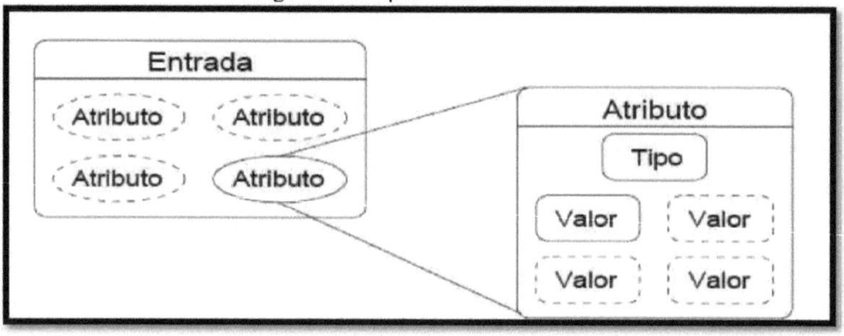

Source: Howes T., "The String Representation of LDAP Search Filters," RFC 2254, December 1997.

Each node corresponds to an entry in the directory.

2.2.7. ATTRIBUTES

By definition, the attributes of each object allow the user to perform a search to find the object without knowing the exact name of the object.

Directory data is represented by attribute pairs and their value. For example the attribute commonName, or cn (first name), is used to store the name of a person. A person named Diego Bastidas can be represented in the directory by:

1. cn: Diego Bastidas

Each person entered in the directory is defined by the collection of attributes in the person object class.

Other attributes:

2. givenname: Diego

3. surname: Bastidas

4. e-mail: dbastidas@brigadagalapagos.com

The required attributes are those that must be present in the entries using the object class. All entries^ precise of the allowed attributes are those that may be present in the entries that use the object class. For example, in the object class person, the attributes cn and sn are required. The attributes description, telephoneNumber, seealso, and userpassword are allowed but not required. Each attribute has a syntax definition that corresponds to it. The syntax definition describes the type of information provided by that attribute:

5. <u>bin</u>: binary

6. <u>ces</u>: case-sensitive string (upper and lower case are significant during comparisons)

7. <u>cis</u>: string with uppercase and lowercase letters ignored (uppercase and lowercase letters are not significant during comparisons)

8. <u>tel</u>: telephone number string (like cis, but during comparisons blanks and dashes "_" are ignored)

9. <u>dn</u>: "distinguished name" (distinguished name)

It is necessary to remember that an attribute is a container that can be used to store a single type of information within your directory.

^Input is a set of several attributes

2.2.8. ATTRIBUTE TYPES

An attribute type definition specifies the syntax of an attribute and how attributes of that type are ordered and compared. The attribute types in the directory form a class tree. For example, the attribute type "commonName" is a subclass of the attribute type "name". There are mandatory and optional attributes listed in the following illustration:

Attribute Identifier Attribute Value Description

NUMERICOID: (required) Unique Object Identifier (OID).

NAME: Attribute Name.

DESC: Attribute Description.

OBSOLETE: "true" if obsolete; "false" or absent if not obsolete.

SUP: Name of the superior attribute type from which the attribute type is derived.

EQUALITY: Name or OID of the matching rule if matching equality is allowed; absent if it is not.

ORDERING: Name or OID of the matching rule if ordering is allowed; absent if it is not.

SUBSTRING: Name or OID of the matching rule if sub-string matching is allowed or absent if it is not.

SYNTAX OID: numeric syntax of the values of this type.

SINGLE-VALUE: "true" if the attribute is not multi-valued; "false" or absent if it is.

COLLECTIVE: "true" if the attribute is collective; "false" or absent if it is not.

NO-USER-MODIFICATION: "true" if the attribute is not user-modifiable; "false" or absent if it is.

USAGE: Description of the use of the attribute.

These attributes correspond to the definition of "AttributeTypeDescription" in RFC 2252.

2.2.9. LDIF

LDIF (RFC 2849) conveys the contents of the directory as a recordset, one record for each object (or entry) representing update requests, such as add, modify, delete, and rename, as a recordset, one record for each update request. The first use of LDIF was in describing directory entries. Later, the format was extended by allowing the representation of changes to directory entries. To import and export directory information between LDAP-based directory servers, or to describe a set of changes to be applied to the directory, the file format known as LDIF (LDAP Interchange Format) is generally used. An LDIF file stores information in object-oriented hierarchies of entries. All LDAP servers include a utility to convert LDIF files to object-oriented format. It is usually an ASCII file.

EXAMPLE:

An ordinary LDIF file looks like this:

dn: uid=djbastidas,ou=People,dc=company,dc=com

uid: djbastidas

cn: Diego Javier Bastidas

objectclass: account

objectclass: posixAccount

objectclass: top

loginshell: /bin/bash

uidnumber: 512

gidnumber: 300

homedirectory: /home/jmsuarez

gecos: Diego Javier Bastidas,,,,

userpassword: {crypt}LPnaOoUYN57Netaac

As can be seen, each entry is identified by a distinctive name:

DN ("*distinguished name*") is composed of the name of the entry in question, plus the path of names that allow the entry to be traced back to the top of the directory hierarchy.

2.2.10. OBJECTS

In LDAP, an object class defines the collection of attributes that can be used to define an entry. The LDAP standard provides these basic types for object classes:

-1-   Groups in the directory, including unordered lists of individual objects or of object groups.
-2-   Locations, such as the name of the country and its description.

-3-	Organizations that are in the directory.

-4-	People who are in the directory.

A given entry can belong to more than one object class. For example, the entry for persons is defined by the object class person, but it can also be defined by attributes in the object classes inetOrgPerson, groupOfNames and oganization. The object class structure a of the server determines the list of required and allowed attributes for a particular entry.

Figure N° 8. Domain Organization

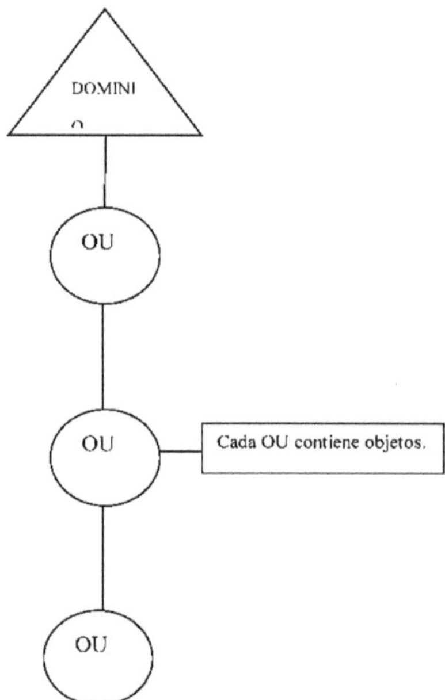

Source: Howes T., and M. Smith, "The LDAP URL Format," RFC 2255, December 1997.

0An object can be any resource in the domain such as files, applications or even users.

2.3. TECHNICAL ASPECTS

LDAP is a protocol for unified access to a set of information about a network at the application layer. When performing a software inventory of the organization. That is, a list of all the programs used in the equipment to be migrated. This will help us to

identify all applications and services. The objective is to determine under these problems, the way in which third parties (attackers) mock the users that operate in a given network, either by interrupting communication, disabling services, manipulating information and producing conflicts in the systems with which they work as well as what is the best solution to the current design of the network and then implement and largely solve the problem of security and connectivity that existed in this network. It is important to emphasize that access to each stage will give us enough information to determine how the network is designed and what its main operating problems are. Once certain important concepts have been clarified, a network diagram can now be drawn up, so access was gained to the Communications Department of BCB GALÁPAGOS where the equipment is located and, with information provided by the network administrator, it was established that the network devices, such as routers and switches, form part of both the modular and fixed physical configurations. Based on the TCP/IP model, a general approach to the vulnerability of each stage can be made, which are detailed below:

2.3.1. NETWORK LAYER

The network layer or network layer, according to OSI standardization, is a level or layer that provides connectivity and route selection between two host systems that may be located in geographically distinct networks. The main drawbacks in this layer may occur if someone has access to the equipment with which the network operates, i.e. access to the Communications Department, the cabling or remote equipment established for communication (attacks on the network layer may be those that occur in cabling lines, diversion of cabling, interception of communication between equipment), which is why the main drawbacks that may occur in this layer are associated with the degree of confidentiality and access control that a person may have or manage. The institution's internal network has a structured cabling system that leaves the computer room and is distributed from the switches to the workstations.

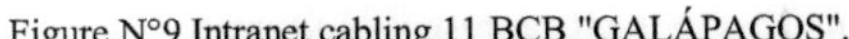

Figure.N°9 Intranet cabling 11 BCB "GALÁPAGOS".

Source: Diego Javier Bastidas Logroño

Unauthorized users are not allowed access to this room, which is an optimal security measure. The key to accessing it is to have access to IP datagrams, which can be found in each packet circulating through the network, by means of spy software. As previously mentioned, the institution's intranet is unprotected, so that if it were decided to obtain any type of information through the use of the Internet protocol, it would be possible to do so.

2.3.2. TRANSPORT LAYER

The transport layer includes the following functions:

-1- Allows multiple applications to communicate on the network at the same time as on a single device.
-2- Ensures that, if necessary, all data is received reliably and in order by the correct application
-3- Employs error handling mechanisms.

The main vulnerabilities are associated with integration authentication and confidentiality. These terms are related to the access to the communication protocols between layers, allowing the denial or manipulation of them, which will be detailed below.

To talk about the security problems that arise from this protocol is undoubtedly to talk about a whole subject, here we will only deal with a few of them, which are of interest and occur in the practical case.

TCP (which stands for *Transmission Control Protocol*) is one of the main protocols of the transport layer of the TCP/IP model. At the application level, it enables the management of data coming from or going to the lowest level of the model (i.e., the IP protocol). When data is provided to the IP protocol, it groups it into IP datagrams, setting the protocol field to 6 (so that it knows in advance that the protocol is TCP). TCP is a connection-oriented protocol, i.e. it allows two communicating machines to control the state of the transmission. This in itself represents a security risk, since being a connection-oriented protocol anything could happen. The search for information on tcp and udp ports (User Datagram Protocol) is a non-connection oriented protocol of the transport layer of the TCP/IP model. This protocol is very simple since it does not provide error detection. These are systems that allow the identification of valid connections, both at the source and at the destination, by means of logical numbers assigned to each type of connection, being able to use or not use the services that a given connection can offer. The condition of use allows a port to have three states: open, closed and blocked. Therefore, by means of the ports it is possible to determine in the first instance the type of service offered by a given device or network. Therefore, knowing these conditions, an analysis can be made based on the possible problems that may exist or the problems that may occur in a port. Each TCP segment has 20 bytes of payload in the header that encapsulates the application layer data, while each UDP segment has only 8 bytes of payload.

The responsibilities to be fulfilled by the transport layer are as follows: **Tracking individual conversations:** any host may have multiple applications communicating across the network. Each of these applications will communicate with one or more applications on remote hosts. It is the responsibility of the transport layer to maintain multiple communication streams between these applications.

Data segmentation: Just as each application creates stream data to be sent to a remote application, this data can be prepared to be sent across media in manageable chunks. Transport layer protocols describe the services that segment this application layer data. This includes the encapsulation required in each data section. Each application data section requires headers to be added at the transport layer to indicate the communication with which it is associated.

Segment reassembly: At the receiving host, each data section can be routed to the appropriate application. In addition, these individual data sections must also be reconstructed to generate a complete data stream that is useful for the application layer. The protocols at the transport layer describe how the header information of the layer is used to reassemble the parts of the data into streams to pass on to the application layer.

Application identification: To pass data streams to the appropriate applications, the transport layer must identify the target application. To accomplish this, the transport layer assigns an identifier to the application. TCP/IP protocols call this identifier a port number. All software processes that require access to the network are assigned a unique port number on that host. This port number is used in the transport layer header to indicate which application is associated with which party.

The transport layer is the link between the application layer and the lower layer that is responsible for network transmission. This layer accepts data from different conversations and passes it on to the lower layers as manageable parts that can eventually be multiplexed in the network. In addition, the lower layers are not aware that there are multiple applications sending data on the network. Their responsibility is to deliver the data to the appropriate device. The transport layer then sorts these parts before sending them to the appropriate application.

2.3.3. APPLICATION LAYER

The LDAP Protocol refers to an application-level protocol that allows access to an ordered and distributed directory service for searching various information in a network environment. The application layer, the seventh layer, is the top layer of the OSI and TCP/IP models. It provides the interface between the applications used to communicate and the underlying network over which messages are transmitted. Application layer protocols are used to exchange data between programs running on the source and destination hosts. Many application layer protocols exist and new protocols are always being developed. The functions associated with application layer protocols allow the human network to communicate with the underlying data network. When we open a Web browser or an instant messaging window, an application is launched, and the program is placed in the memory of the device where it runs. Each executable program loaded onto a device is called a process. Within the application layer, there are two forms of processes or software programs that provide access to the network: applications and services.

Network-aware applications: Applications are the software programs that people use to communicate over the network. Some end-user applications are network-aware, which means that they implement application layer protocols and can communicate directly with the lower layers of the protocol stack. E-mail clients and Web browsers are examples of such applications.

Application layer services: Other programs may need the help of application layer services to use network resources, such as file transfer or print queuing on the network. Although transparent to the user, these services are the programs that communicate with the network and prepare the data for transfer. Different types of data, whether text, graphics or video, require different network services to ensure that they are well prepared to process the functions of the lower layers of the OSI model. Each network service or application uses protocols that define the standards and data formats to be used. Without protocols, the data network would not have a common way of formatting and addressing data. It is necessary to become familiar with the underlying protocols that govern the operation of the different network services to understand their function. The Application layer provides applications with the ability to access the services of the other layers and defines the protocols used by applications to exchange data. It should be clarified that the user does not normally interact directly with the application layer, but usually interacts with programs that in turn interact with the application layer but hide the underlying complexity.

The application layer is responsible for direct access to the underlying processes that manage and send communication to the human network. This layer serves as the source and destination for communications over data networks. The applications, protocols and services of the application layer allow users to interact with the data network in a meaningful and efficient way. Protocols provide a structure of agreed-upon rules and processes that ensure that services running on a particular device can send and receive data from a variety of different network devices.

2.4. CONCEPTUAL FOUNDATION

Attacker: A person who wishes to obtain information to visualize, investigate and analyze, and then, based on the analysis, make an attack or contribution to the system.

Peering Over Your Shoulder Attack: Means that an unauthorized user, whether a friend of the computer user or not, snoops around and without the user's knowledge while you are present steals important information by "peering over your shoulder".

Binding: In computer science, a binding is a "binding" or reference to another, longer, more complicated and frequently used symbol. This other symbol can be a value of any type, numeric, string, or the name of a variable containing a value or a set of values.

Header: It is part of a data packet and allows validation and control of the packets sent through the network.

TTL field: Allows to determine the time in the transmission of data packets, limiting them to a certain time if necessary.

Client: A client is a computer system that remotely accesses a service on another computer by accessing the network.

DNS (Domain Name System): This is the Internet's naming service and is used to map fully qualified (easy to remember) names to IP addresses.

Routers: Allows routing and filtering of data flowing through the network.

Encapsulation: The process by which data is wrapped in a particular protocol header.

Cache Frame Poisoning: Method that allows to perform adulteration in the MAC.

Finger: Tool to identify the number of users and their names.

GQ: ldap client application

GUI: Graphical User Interface.

GTK: A set of cross-platform libraries for developing graphical user interfaces.

Host: Device that communicates over a network.

Spatial indicators (Flags): TCP protocol element that uses 6 bits to enable or disable login on TCP ports.

LDAP (Free Directory Access Protocol): Standard for directory services. It is a light version of DAP (Directory Access Protocol) that is part of X.500 and is built to run over TCP/IP.

OSI Model: Defines the communications process completely, and divides it into clearly demarcated functions and names those functions, its layers are: Physical, Data Link, Network, Transport, Session,

Presentation, Application.

Multiplexing: Division of data into smaller data units to improve transmission speed.

Networking: Generally the term NETWORKING is applied to the integration of two complete network systems, its main objective being to make all its programs, data and equipment available to anyone on the network who requests it, regardless of the physical location of the resource and the user.

NIS (Network Information System): Developed by SUN and allows users to access files and applications on many hosts using a single ID and Passwords.

Packets: A set of data that is transmitted over a network.

Gateway: Device that allows interconnecting networks with different protocols and architectures and whose purpose is to translate the information of the protocol used in a network to the protocol used in the destination network.

Default policy: It is the condition acquired by an equipment according to its configuration, to accept or deny certain conditions.

TCP sequence prediction: Method that simulates the participation in a network, allowing access to a particular network and managing to steal a TCP session.

Protocol: A set of rules governing communication.

Proxy: A program or device that performs an Internet access task in place of another computer. It is an intermediate point between a computer connected to the Internet and the server it is accessing.

P2P: Peer-to-peer networking in which computers that are part of the same network create a distribution system. It is mostly used to share files with other p2p peers. Peer-to-peer computing requires each network device to run both the client and server sides of an application.

Ports: Ports are typically used to identify a particular process or service on a computer. When a remote device wants to access a certain service on a server, for example, it directs that data to a particular port that identifies the type of service the device wants to use.

External Network: It is the global computer network.

Internal Network: It is a particular network of an organization that is separated from the global network, becoming a more private network.

Segments: These are Messages in different sizes.

Server: Equipment that provides services to clients. Servers are the central point in client/server model networks. There are many services that a server can provide to network clients. For example DNS, DHCP, file storage, application hosting, Web site hosting, Ldap, etc.

Sniffing: Information gathering process by means of software.

Sniffers: Process of interception of information in the network that can later allow, through the use of software, the capture, analysis and interpretation of datagrams circulating in a network.

SSL/TLS: Secure Sockets Layer (SSL; secure socket layer protocol) and its predecessor Transport Layer Security (TLS; transport layer security) are cryptographic protocols that provide secure communications over a network, commonly the Internet.

Stream : The continuous transmission of data from one location to another.

Suse Linux: SUSE includes a unique installation and administration program called YaST2 that allows you to perform updates, configure the network and firewalls, manage users, and many more options all integrated into a single user-friendly interface.

TCP/IP : Transmission Control Protocol/Internet Protocol. Common name for the protocol suite developed by the U.S. DoD in the 1970s to enable the creation of globally interconnected networks. TCP and IP are the two best-known protocols in the suite.

Network Address Translation (NAT): A mechanism that allows data packets to be exchanged between two networks that assign incompatible addresses to each other.

UDP: (User Datagram Protocol) is a non-connection-oriented protocol of the transport layer of the TCP/IP model.

CHAPTER III

3. ANALYSIS AND INTERPRETATION OF RESULTS

The data presented in this study were commonly accepted observing an acceptance in the surveys conducted to computer users within the network of the BRIGADA DE CABALLERÍA BLINDADA No. 11 GALÁPAGOS.

The survey questions and their respective result is the following to test if it is a feasible project to the users regarding the implementation of the LDAP protocol.

1. For security reasons would you like to authenticate yourself with a name and password on your computer before logging in?

Figure.No.10 Survey, Question N° 1

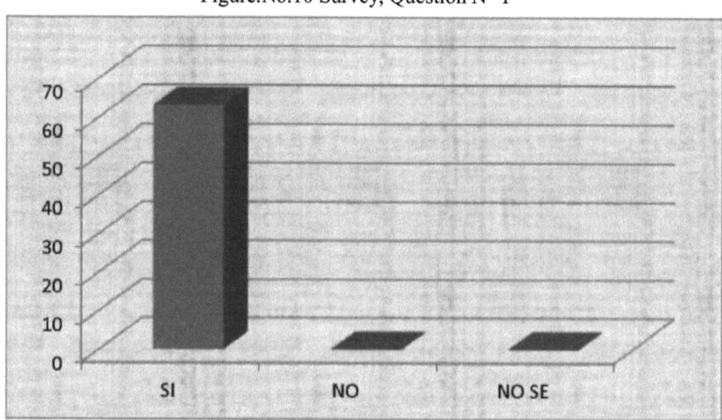

Source: Diego Javier Bastidas Logroño

YES: 63 UsersNo   : 0 Users Unsure: 0 Users

100% of military and public service personnel believe that the implementation of the LDAP protocol would improve their performance in the face of new computer security techniques and security against unauthorized access to their computers with their personal and non-transferable username and password.

2. Why if the answer is yes?
    1. For security against unauthorized access = 33 Users
    2. For the Look over the shoulder attack =30 Users

Figure.No.11 Survey, Question No. 2

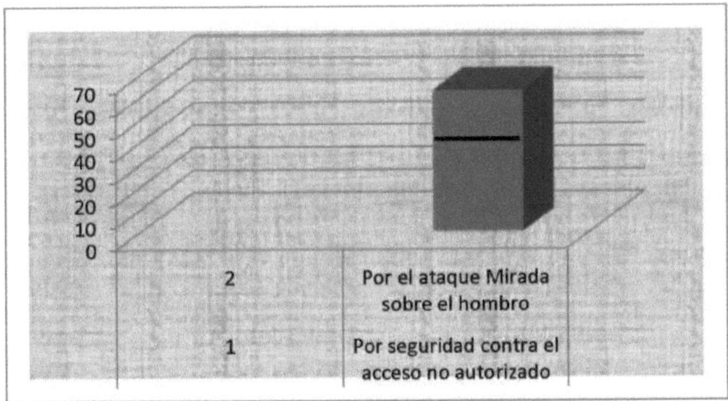

Source: Diego Javier Bastidas Logroño

52% (33 Users) of military and public service personnel believe that the implementation of the LDAP protocol would improve their performance and would not allow unauthorized users unauthorized access to the Institution's valuable information, 48% (30 Users) believe that the implementation of the LDAP protocol would improve their performance and would prevent the Look Over Your Shoulder attack.

3. Why if the answer is negative?

There are no negative responses.

0%   (0 Users) of military and public service personnel believe that the implementation of the LDAP protocol would improve its performance and it does not plan to stop implementing it for a moment.

4. Why is it important to you that the information on your computer is not altered or lost?

1.   In order not to cause institutional instability =33 Users

2.   To avoid having to repeat the work =30 Users

Figure.No.12Survey, Question N° 4

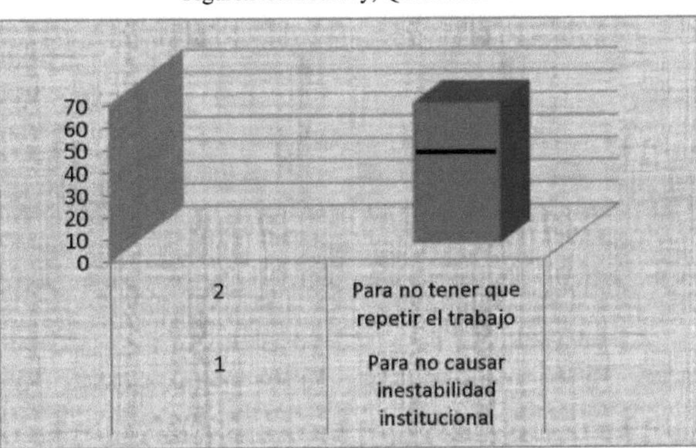

Source: Diego Javier Bastidas Logroño

52% (33 Users) of military and public service personnel consider that the implementation of the LDAP protocol would improve their performance and would not allow institutional instability when information is altered or lost, 48% (30 Users) consider that the implementation of the LDAP protocol would improve their performance and would avoid having to repeat the work done in case the information is altered or lost.

5. What benefits would you see for the institution in implementing the LDAP protocol to implement the above mentioned services?

1. Keep unauthorized users out of the network = 26 Users

2. Maintain a secure authentication process with a unique user name and non-transferable password = 37 Users

Figure.No.13Survey, Question No. 5

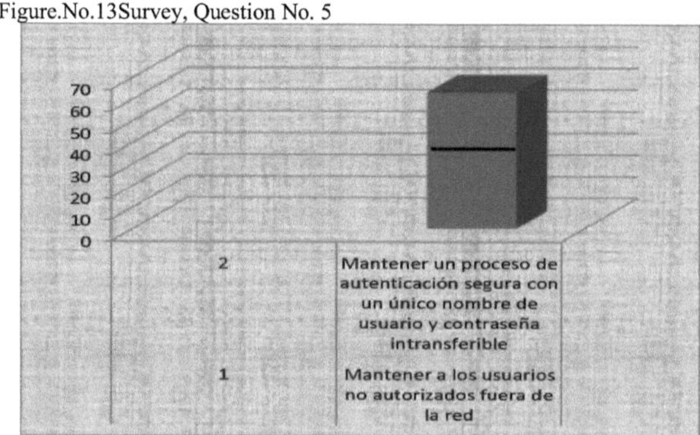

Source: Diego Javier Bastidas Logroño

41% (26 Users) of military and public service personnel believe that implementing the LDAP protocol would improve their performance and would not allow unauthorized access to unauthorized personnel on the data network.

59% (37 Users) consider that the implementation of the LDAP protocol would improve their performance and maintain a secure authentication process with a single non-transferable username and password.

5. Would you like to prevent the look-over-the-shoulder attack by implementing this LDAP protocol?

Figure.No.14 Survey, Question N° 6

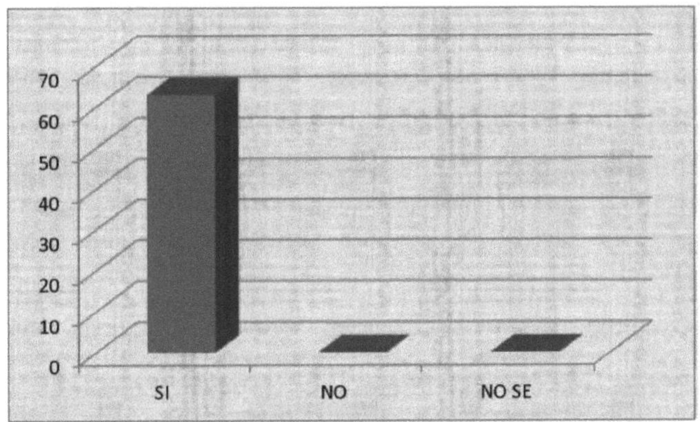

Source: Diego Javier Bastidas Logroño

51: 63 UsersNo   : 0 Users Unsure: 0 Users

100% of military and public service personnel believe that implementing the LDAP protocol would improve their performance in the face of new computer security techniques and prevent the Look on the shoulder attack.

The investigative improvement of personnel in learning to manage Linux and Windows applications has direct testing mechanisms, however, we will try to quantify the degree of the same based on all parameters and indicators that can be evaluated. A non-statistical technique based on percentages will be used. A high percentage in the results of the academic research TEST will define a high degree of improvement. While a low percentage will reflect a null or almost null improvement. The following scale can be used:

- Absolute improvement (100%): The implementation of the LDAP protocol in the establishment of a domain with reliable open source for both Linux and Windows shows a 100% increase in research activity.

• High degree of improvement (80% - 99%) - The implementation of the LDAP protocol in the establishment of a domain controller with reliable open source (suse) for both Linux and Windows with all its features presented platforms and technologies that are compatible with various operating systems that have to be reviewed before starting a practical implementation.

Low improvement (50% - 59%) - the platforms and technologies used are compatible only in certain aspects with the new operating systems under test, such as Windows.

3.1. PROJECT RESULTS

The main result of the project is a powerful and flexible tool, within the framework of an Open Source platform, capable of maintaining the Free Directory Access Protocol on SUSE Linux in its current version, with the application of GQ and yast administration, all the necessary information and instructions for each authenticated user on the network in the establishment of a reliable domain for Windows and Linux.

Once the user is authenticated, the user can access the resources that the administrator allows. The authentication process contains an interactive connection, where the user types a valid domain name and local computer password that confirms the user's identity to any network service the user accesses. Throughout its volume of computer security technical presentations have been developed with a focus on the subject of LDAP project has the ability to continuously update, delete, enter their users from the server according to the need or institutional changes that usually take effect. This implementation of the LDAP protocol will contribute greatly to the institutional development required by the BRIGADA DE CABALLERÍA BLINDADA No. 11 "GALÁPAGOS".

The client establishes a TCP/IP session with the LDAP server. This operation is always accompanied by the client's binding to the LDAP server's directory, so these two operations are often referred to as binding from the client to the LDAP server. The establishment of a session implies that the LDAP client must specify the IP address or name of the server, as well as the TCP port over which the LDAP service is available. Then in the binding to the directory, the client must provide a username and password for authentication to gain access to the appropriate permissions and access for the execution of the tasks in the following section.

-1-   The client performs one or more search (read) or update operations on the directory. These operations are those seen in the LDAP Functional Model section. The client receives the results of its operation from the server. Each of these results is received in separate messages, hence LDAP is a message-oriented protocol. In addition to this, the client receives a result code of the operation from the server.

   -I- The client terminates and disconnects from the server.

The LDAP protocol also allows the client to perform more than one operation at a time, in which case each message from the server will have a code that specifies the operation to which the message belongs. The clients are then authenticated within the tree and domain to which each of them belongs, and the administrator can edit, create, update, delete the information required by the institution as needed. The importance of security in network environments cannot be underestimated, over the years the evasion of computer attacks has been increasingly complicated, that is why the new challenge of implementing the LDAP protocol in the establishment of a reliable domain for Windows and Linux has become feasible to prevent unauthorized access to information by unauthorized people to information of the 11 B.C.B. GALÁPAGOS.

3.2. DISCUSSION

The main reason why many LDAP servers exist is because the network must be able to deny access to unauthorized people, it is a means of security for the client, another security factor is the authentication of network users, as the network must keep unauthorized users out of it, authorized users must be able to securely access the network with password control to the most appropriate computer to safeguard and protect data and information. Finally, authenticated users must be able to access network resources. This issue in itself can be complicated since each user needs access to certain resources to perform his or her work, while others do not. In practice, the implementation of the LDAP protocol in the establishment of a domain with reliable open source for both Linux and Windows will operate if the following conditions are met:

-2-   Common transport mechanisms (ipv6 - ipv4).

-3-   LAN and/or WAN network environment, etc.

-4-   Compatible version of SUSE with Windows.

-5-   Compatible version of GQ and yast.

-6-   LDAP compatible version.

-7-   Linux Security Certificates

User management is the activity referred to the creation and maintenance of user accounts, among its main characteristics are:

-8-   User registrations, cancellations and modifications in the network.

-9-   Establishment of password policies such as password length, password lifetime, password database security.

-10-   Assignment of permissions for the use of network resources.

3.3. CONCLUSIONS

-1-   The administration of Linux servers is one of the most important tasks within a company and institution since the implementation of the free directory access protocol will help in the secure authentication of users.

-2-   In terms of security, it should be the first option given its openness and being able to know how the tools are made, with the completion of this project several questions were solved, such as preventing the loss of information of the institution with the Look over the Shoulder attack.

-3-   The implementation of the Free Directory Access Protocol provided a solution to the problems of information security for each user on the network, in addition to creating the LDAP domain tree.

3.4. RECOMMENDATIONS

-1-It is recommended to perform this type of research and implementation on other corporate networks. In the public and private sector where there are no computer security policies, which becomes urgent as most institutions since the handling of information is precious.

-2-The implementation of firewall rules must be in accordance with the security policies of each institution and its connectivity needs. It is advisable to inquire about this to those in charge of administration, since the look-over-the-shoulder attack with LDAP user authentication has been discarded.

-3-At the time of making an implementation such as the one carried out by the BRIGADA DE CABALLERÍA BLINDADA No.11 "GALÁPAGOS", it should be done together with the system administrators, because new technology is used, and its subsequent administration will depend on them, therefore it is advisable to be informed at all times of the changes made and how the process is being carried out. In addition, it is important to emphasize that you must ask for their collaboration because the benefit will be for the users of the same institution.

CHAPTER IV

4. PROPOSITIONAL FRAMEWORK

The implementation of a Domain with the LDAP protocol and its application in the establishment of a domain with free software under Linux and its application in the BRIGADA DE CABALLERÍA BLINDADA No.11 GALÁPAGOS will allow the creation of a reliable authentication domain for both Windows and Linux in addition to providing computer security especially for the Look over the Shoulder attack.

4.1. PRESENTATION

Due to the lack of security in the accesses of the clients to each computer, also to the loss of important information that could occur with several computer attacks especially the one of Looking over the shoulder, someone can have access to the information not being authorized, which can be expensive in the long term. In order to perform the analysis of a secure network, it is necessary to know the details and characteristics of the underlying communications protocols, which will be in charge of transporting the information and data to be distributed. At the same time, the services provided in the network and their operating details must be analyzed. In this work we have opted for an eminently technical approach to the existing vulnerabilities from a practical point of view, taking as a practical case the implementation of the ldap protocol in the data network of the BRIGADA DE CABALLERÍA BLINDADA No.11 GALÁPAGOS. With a practical view provided by the existing tools of the implementation of the Free Directory Access Protocol to allow or deny the execution of the mentioned vulnerabilities. It contains more descriptive and attribute-based information than a database. The information contained in a directory is read much more than it is written. As a result, directories do not normally implement the complicated transaction schemas or rollback schemas that databases use to perform complex updates of large volumes of data. When directory information is duplicated, temporary inconsistencies between the information in the replicas can be accepted, as long as there is eventually synchronization. There are many different ways of providing a directory service. The different methods make it possible to store different types of information in the directory, establish different requirements for referencing, querying and updating information, the way in which the directory is protected from unauthorized access. The LDAP directory service is based on a client-server model as stated above. One or more LDAP servers contain the data that makes up the LDAP directory tree. The ldap client connects to the LDAP server and queries it. The server responds with a corresponding answer, or with an indication of where the client can find more information (usually another LDAP server). No matter which LDAP server the client connects to, it will always see the same directory view; the name presented to one LDAP server refers to the same entry that it would refer to on another LDAP server. This is an important feature of a universal directory service such as LDAP.

4.2. OBJECTIVES

The general objective of the project is to implement an LDAP directory system in the BRIGADA DE CABALLERÍA BLINDADA No.11 "GALÁPAGOS", so that each user has a directory associated with individual authentication.

The specific objectives of the project are listed below:

-1-   Install, configure and start up an LDAP directory server.

-2-   Populate the directories of such a server with the information of each user.

-3-   To provide security to users against the Look Over the Shoulder attack.

-4-   To provoke the current administrators to reanalyze the security of the

directory and can also serve as a guide for administrators who are taking on this task for the first time.

4.3. CONTENT OF THE PROPOSAL

4.3.1. LDAP SOLUTIONS

As is well known, designing is a very subjective task. There are many different ways to assess business needs and design network solutions. However, in all cases, this process can be divided into three phases:

-1-   Design.

-2-   Implementation

-3-   Administration.

Figure. No. 15 Phases for network solutions.

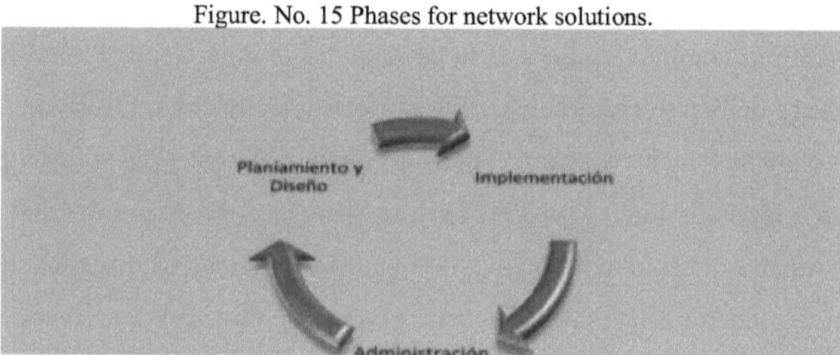

Source: Source Pyme Instituto Tecnológico Informática, Daniel Sáez

As you can see this is a never ending process. It starts with Design, Implementation and then moves on to Management, while Management will move on to Design again. This section deals with the design and planning phase. It will discuss the analysis process and the design for the LDAP project of the armored cavalry brigade No.11 "GALAPAGOS", which, based on functionality, will be divided into four sections. Some of these sections are independent, while others are dependent.

4.3.2. DESIGN

In this section, depending on the services required, the protocol suite will be chosen. The TCP/IP suite works with a wide variety of physical networks, therefore, it is the only protocol that can meet the requirements of the project BRIGADA DE CABALLERÍA BLINDADA No.11 "GALÁPAGOS".

Before starting our network design, the following needs to be decided

    1. The need for Network Services.

Increasing network complexity demonstrates the need for a centrally managed automatic IP configuration regime. The *Dynamic Host Configuration Protocol* (DHCP) in Linux provides an automated and centralized system of IP addressing services managed and granted via TCP/IP.
DHCP allows hosts on the network to acquire IP address and optional TCP/IP client information from a DHCP server. As mentioned in the previous point, the BRIGADA DE CABALLERÍA BLINDADA No. 11 "GALÁPAGOS" has an internet provider: CNT (Corporación Nacional de Telecomunicaciones), with a contracted bandwidth of 2MB respectively. The network domain is called BRIGADA DE CABALLERÍA BLINDADA NO.11 "GALÁPAGOS" and most of the workstations are linked to this domain (the rest are not but they work normally). It has a server for the network: CLEAR OS operating system as domain controller, the addressing is done manually, i.e. there is no DHCP server, and the addresses are assigned without any special order, there is no restriction for users to prevent users from accessing any gateway, there is no firewall, nor the LDAP requirement that is so necessary for the integrity of the institution's data.

Figure. N°16 Network Diagram of the 11 BCB "GALÁPAGOS".

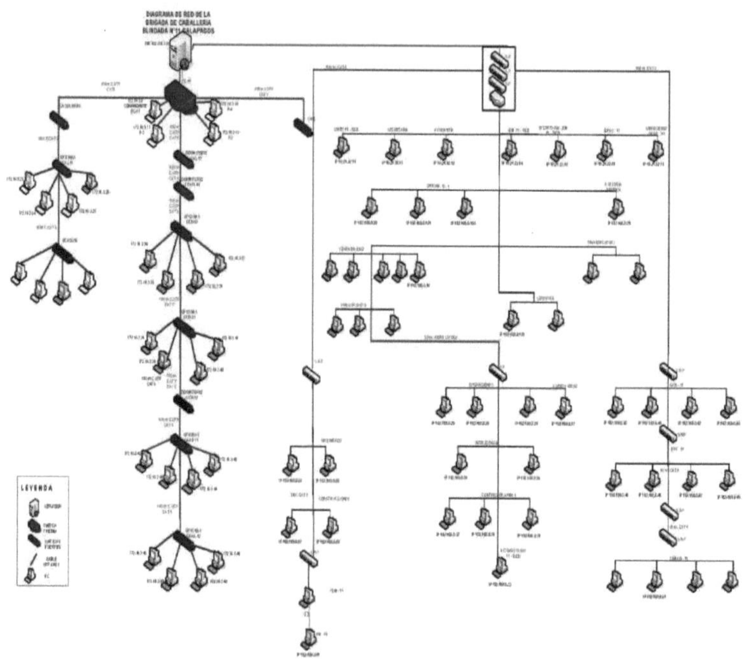

Source: Armored Cavalry Brigade No.11 "Galapagos".

4.3.3. USER IMPLEMENTATION

When implemented with the GQ tool and yast on SUSE running on a graphical environment, developed with the GTK libraries, it allows us to manage the OpenLDAP directory. Normally available as a package in some GNU/Linux distributions.

Very handy for managing the directory and user accounts in graphical mode, as well as reading entries. GQ will also allow you to add entries using existing entries as templates. By linking to the LDAP server with loop dn, you can add, edit and delete GUI entries.

The domain controller contains a database of all the users and machines that are part of our network, this way we can manage resources and security policies in a centralized way and this allows us to have a more secure and comfortable environment to work in. For an openSUSE server configured as a primary domain controller using the ldapsam backend, the nmb, smb and ldap services must be running, and the dhcpd service must also be running if the server provides DHCP services. For an openSUSE machine that is a member of a Samba Domain, the winbind service must be running, if you want to share resources with other machines, the smb and nmb services must also be running, when mounting network shares on your openSUSE 11.2 workstation, the smfs service must be up and the nscd service must be down.

The users configured in the server as explained above are divided by each Armed Group with its respective name, each Armed Group is dedicated to a specific function in this prestigious national security institution.

Table .No. 1 Users

GROUP GCB31 MACHALA			
FUNCTION	**AMANUENSES**	**USER**	**IP**
COMMANDER31	commandergcb31	llomas	10.21.32.40
2nd COMMANDER31	2cmdtegcb31	fmanosalvas	10.21.32.41
PERSONNEL31	personalgcb31	Ssary	10.21.32.42
FIXED ASSETS31	fixedassetsgcb31	jallauca	10.21.32.43
OPERATIONS31	operationsgcb31	tnovillo	10.21.32.44
LOGISTICS31	logisticagcb31	ssagnay	10.21.32.45
COMMUNICATIONS31	communicationsgcb31	Yrogel	10.21.32.46
armored reconnaissance squadron no. 11 epiclachima			
FUNCTION	**AMANUENSES**	**USER**	**IP**
COMANDANTEERS	cmdteersll	Vrocha	10.21.32.47
PERSONALERS	personalersll	Jjimenez	10.21.32.48
INTELLIGENCE	intelligenceersll	Mnaranjo	10.21.32.49
OPERATIONS	operacionesersll	ryumisaca	10.21.32.50
LOGISTICAERS	logisticaersll	Lsanchez	10.21.32.51
COMMUNICATIONS	communications	centralersll	10.21.32.52
EEB11 ENGINEERING GROUP			

FUNCTION	AMANUENSES	USER	IP
COMMANDEREEB	commandereebll	Kalmeida	10.21.32.60
2nd COMMANDEREEB	2cmdteeeb11	msantacruz	10.21.32.61
CONSTRUCTIONSEEB	constructionseebll	Lmate	10.21.32.62
MEETING ROOMSEEB	salaleebll	salal	10.21.32.63
MEETINGSEEB	room2eeb11	room2	10.21.32.64
PERSONALEEB	personaleebll	oshamingui	10.21.32.65
INTELLIGENCEEEB	intelligenceeebll	Wobando	10.21.32.66
OPERATIONSEEB	operationseebll	Jzaruma	10.21.32.67
LOGISTICAEEB	logisticaeebll	Ngodoy	10.21.32.68

POLICE M 11

FUNCTION	AMANUENSES	USER	IP
PERSONNELALEPM	personalepmll	Cfreire	10.21.32.69
OPERATIONSEPM	operationsepmll	rmaldonado	10.21.32.70
MUSICOS11			
PERSONALEBM	personalebmll	jorozco	10.21.32.71
OPERATIONSEBM	operationsebmll	jcastillo	10.21.32.72
FISCAL HOUSING	viviendafiscalllbcb	Fcastro	10.21.32.73

CEMABLIN GROUP 11BCB

FUNCTION	AMANUENSES	USER	IP
CEMABLIN	Cmdtecemab	kcarrera	10.21.32.78

2CMDTECEMAB11	2cmdtecemab	mcisneros	10.21.32.79
STAFF	Personalcemab	fdicado	10.21.32.80
FIXED ASSETS	Assetsfij oscemab	erojan	10.21.32.81
MAINTENANCE	Mttocemab	ralvarez	10.21.32.82
LOGISTICS	Logisticacemab	Mdiaz	10.21.32.83
B. TOOLS	Toolscemab	jnarvaez	10.21.32.84
AULA	Instruccioncemab	jordoñez	10.21.32.85
COSINA	ranchero11bcb	dcalderon	10.21.32.86

COMMAND 11BCB			
FUNCTION	**AMANUENSES**	**USER**	**IP**
CMDTE-11-BCB	commander11bcb	enarvaez	10.21.32.5
JEM-11	elderstates11bcb	smorales	10.21.32.6
SECRETARY-11 -BCB	Secretary	dchacon	10.21.32.7
ASSISTANT 11-BCB	edecan11bcb	jchuquimarca	10.21.32.8
SECRETARY -JEM	Secretariajem	mcordova	10.21.32.9
B-1 COMMANDERB1	chiefstaff11bcb	adavalos	10.21.32.10
PERSONNEL SYSTEM	siper11bcb	Lcolcha	10.21.32.11
PART UNITS	parts11bcb	Lcarpio	10.21.32.12
DOCUMENTATION UNITS	documentation11bcb	jvillavicencio	10.21.32.13

INTELLIGENCE			
FUNCTION	**AMANUENSES**	**USER**	**IP**

B-2 COMMANDER B2	chiefintelligence11bcb	jmontenegro	10.21.32.14
SECURITYB2	safetyb2	Eromero	10.21.32.15
SECURITYINTE	internalsecurityb2	ivalenzuela	10.21.32.16
SECURITYEXT	Securityissue	Fcarrera	10.21.32.17

OPERATIONS			
FUNCTION	**AMANUENSES**	**USER**	**IP**
B-3 COMMANDER B3	chiefoperationsllbcb	pponce	10.21.32.18
PLANS AND ORDERS	Plansorders	wcarrasco	10.21.32.19
INSTRUCTION11	instructionllbcb	jyuquilema	10.21.32.20
INSTRUCTION 1	Regulations	wramirez	10.21.32.21
SEPRACSO11BCB	sepracllbcb	Pprieto	10.21.32.22
MARATHON	Physical education	Lreal	10.21.32.23
PROPERTIES	assetsfijosllbcb	Evivas	10.21.32.24
DLINK	operationsroomllbcb	Inaranjo	10.21.32.1
BLINDADA	saltmeetingsllbcb	Sasqui	10.21.32.34

LOGISTICS			
FUNCTION	**AMANUENSES**	**USER**	**IP**
B-4 COMMANDER B4	jefelogisticallbcb	lestrella	10.21.32.25
BRIGADE LOGISTICS	logisticallbcb	azambrano	10.21.32.26
ACQUISITION	acquisitionllbcb	mlozano	10.21.32.27

COST	financellbcb	cfalconez	10.21.32.28
LAWS	lawyerollbcb	gguerra	10.21.32.29
PROCEDURE	Subsidies	vvalencia	10.21.32.30
B-5 OPSIC 11-BCB	Comunicacionsocial	jsalazar	10.21.32.31
JOURNAL	News	Flowers	10.21.32.32
VIDEO	Photography	dcostales	10.21.32.33

4.3.2.1.   TREE DIAGRAM OF THE 11 B.C.B. "GALAPAGOS

They are written in the same way as domains, i.e. from right to left, and are configured as an inverted tree with different branches depending on their intended use.

See **ANNEX 2.**

4.4. PROXY SERVER

Providing Internet access to private network users, while protecting the private network resources from unauthorized users, and to provide additional functions to improve the security, availability and performance of the Internet connectivity solution. For this project, a Squid server is the recommended server to meet the following requirements.

- Restrict Internet and private network traffic.
- Caching HTTP requests
- HTTP request filtering.

4.5. HARDWARE LIMITATIONS:

The network of the BRIGADA DE CABALLERÍA BLINDADA No. 11 "GALÁPAGOS" has a series of limitations at the Hardware level, for which the following equipment had to be acquired as a minimum to be able to carry out the implementation. The following is a list of the missing hardware.

- Two 10/100/1000 Mbps LAN network cards
- One 24-port 100 Mbps switch

4.5.1. HARDWARE COMPATIBILITY

The following requirements should be met to ensure optimal operation of openSUSE :

-Pentium* III 500 MHz or higher (Pentium 4 2.4 GHz or higher or any AMD64 / Intel* EM64T processor recommended)

-Main memory: 512 MB of physical RAM (1 GB recommended)

Hard disk: 3 GB free space (more recommended)

4.5.2. HARDWARE REQUIREMENTS

The following information represents the minimum hardware requirements for the operation of the system, which are provided by 11 B.C.B. GALÁPAGOS.

CPU

- Intel Pentium Core 2 Duo, I3, I5, I7
- AMD 64*2
- **Memory**
- Minimum 4 GB for server
- Recommended 8 GB, for speed

Hard Disk

- 1 TERA byte SERVER installation recommended.

4.5.3. SELECTED TEAMS

The network of the BRIGADA DE CABALLERÍA BLINDADA NO. 11 GALÁPAGOS has two machines that acted as servers for our implementation, each one with optimal characteristics for the correct operation and development of the installed system.

Two of the following equipment were used:

- **HP ProLiant ML370 G4 Server.**
- **CPU:** Intel Core2Duo with 3.2 GB
- **Memory:** 4 GB expandable to 8
- **HARD DISK:** 1 TERA byte
- **Network:** 3 x 10/100/1000 MB Network Cards
- **DVD-ROM** Multi Recorder

4.6. ADMINISTRATION

Server administration is the main and most time-consuming task for system administrators. Open Source offers high performance and networking solutions using new technologies, protocols and the ubiquity of the Internet. Servers with the SUSE Linux Operating System provide a scalable system that offers reliable and fast services to provide greater security, and a standard service in automated administrative tasks.

4.7. NETWORK AUTHENTICATION

Each user is identified by a user name and the assigned attributes are the password, the access permissions, the workgroups to which he/she belongs, the password expiration date. This system will receive a query each time the user accesses the network and one more each time he/she accesses the workgroup resources (shared directories, printers...) to check the user's permissions. In the face of these hundreds of queries, only a few times a user's password is changed or the user is included in a new workgroup.

4.7.1. OPERATING SYSTEM CONFIGURATION

Here are some suggestions for an optimal installation on any Linux: We choose a simple installation, only with the essential add-ons, when updating the operating system with the latest patches or service packs (ex: sunsolve.sun.com, redhat.com, windowsupdate.microsoft.com..), we choose a suitable file system, usually: Ext3 for Linux. By stopping all services and daemons that are not going to be used, the server is secured and the operating system parameters are optimized.

4.8. FEASIBILITY STUDY

We refer to the availability of the necessary resources to carry out the indicated goals, such as the updating and improvement of services to clients or users, the feasibility will be based on three basic aspects: operative, technical and economic.

4.8.1. OPERATIONAL FEASIBILITY

This refers to the existence of trained personnel required to carry out the project, as well as the existence of end users willing to use the products or services generated by the developed project.

The support from the administration of the Communications and Systems Squadron has been optimal due to the support in the technological and scientific research to find the way to apply the LDAP protocol, the users will only have to remember their user names and passwords respectively to enter their computers. The users have participated in the operational feasibility by means of their help with the Surveys carried out to them, manifesting in the same ones to this one, like a feasible project. The proposed system will not cause any harm as it does not require any knowledge unknown to the administrators since the tests have been done with them. The productivity of the employees will be more reliable after installing the LDAP protocol since the users will be more secure with the information.

Those responsible for the production of the technical management of the communications department, systems and telematics of the Server in which the members of the administration of the network infrastructure and my person in charge of training and implementation of the protocol are synthesized. In addition, each user of the 11 B.C.B. "GALÁPAGOS" of each client computer will be in charge of accessing their information as well as being responsible for remembering their username and password, otherwise you should ask for advice from the server administrators.

The estimated time to complete this project is detailed below using the Gantt chart.

Figure. N° 17 Gantt Chart

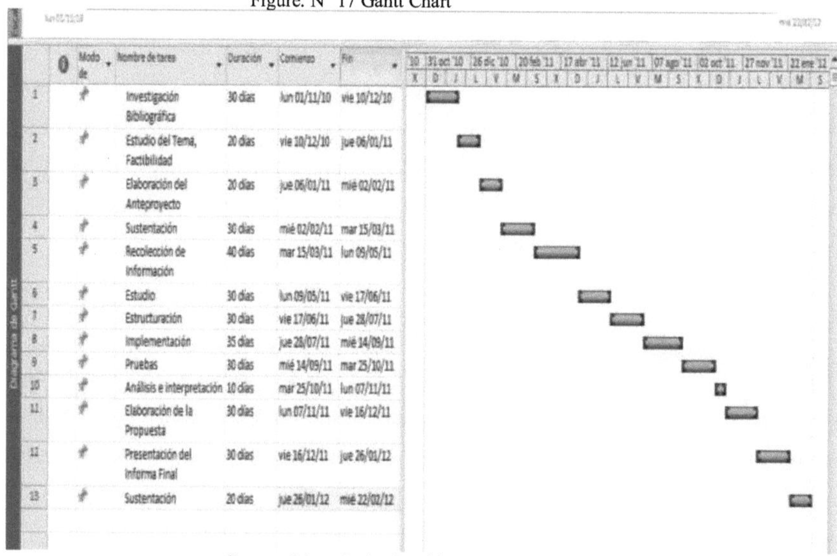

Source: Diego Javier Bastidas Logroño

PERCENTAGE ESTIMATE OF WORK ON THIS PROJECT

1-   LOGICAL DESIGN

a-Analyst   50%.

b-Programmer   25%

c-	Graphic designer 25%.

2-CODIFICATION

a-Analyst	40%.

b-Programmer	30%

c-	Graphic designer 30%.

3-TESTING

a-Analyst	35%.

b-Programmer35% b-Programmer35% b-Programmer

c-	Graphic designer 30%.
4-MAINTENANCE

a-Analyst	45%.

b-Programmer	35

c-	Graphic designer 20% c- Graphic designer 20% c- Graphic designer 20% c- Graphic designer
5-IMPLEMENTATION

a-Analyst	50%.

b-Programmer	50%

6-TRAINING

a-Analyst 100%

4.8.2. TECHNICAL FEASIBILITY

The technological equipment for the implementation of this project is within reach since the hardware to be used in the 11 B.C.B. GALÁPAGOS is available, the implementation of the LDAP protocol will provide adequate responses to requests regardless of the number and location of users as long as it is connected to the network. By implementing the LDAP protocol, it is easy to grow because if more users are added to the network, only more users would be configured on the server and a password and user name would be provided to them.

The tangible technological equipment and software to be used is:

4.8.2.1.1.HARDWARE:

-I-A   number of 2 workstations dedicated to the development and maintenance of the Project, with the following characteristics:

-HP ProLiant ML370 G4 servers.

-CPU   : Intel Core2Duo of 3.2 GB

-Memory   : 4 GB expandable to 8 GB

-DVD-Rw   Multi Recorder

-1 Tera Byte Hard Disk   Drive

-I-Four   100 /1000 Mbps network cards.

-I-Monitor   LCD 32".

-I-Two   100/1000 Mbpswireless Cards.

-I-Mouse   .

-I-Keyboard   .

    -Sophisticated I-UPS.

Other Equipment

-I-One Touch 7100 USB Scanner.

-I-HP 1560 printer.

-LX-300   printer.

-I-Cyber   roam 500.

    -I-Five Dlink Routers.

    -I-Five Cisco Routers: 3 Catalyst 6509 Series.

    -I-Five dlink routers: 6 dir 600 wireless.

    -I-Various dlink switches.

Each customer has at his disposal a computer with the following features

-I-CPU. Intel Dual Core processor.

    -I-Hard Disk   80 gb, Memory 1 Gb, Network Card 100mbps.

-I-LCD Display and RCT 18 Keyboard, Mouse, Speakers, Hp 1560 Printer.

4.8.2.2. SOFTWARE

-1-   Current LinuxSUSE Operating System.

-2-   GQ application.

-3-   Open Source to investigate (Useyast).

-4-   Open Office.

-5-   Vm Ware Virtualizer.

-6-   Mozilla Firefox 9.0 browser.

-7-   Operating System Windows XP Professional service pack 2.

-8-   Operating System Windows 7 ultimate.

-9-   Graphic and multimedia editors: Adobe Illustrator 9.0, Photo Scape, Corel Draw X5, Adobe Photoshop CS4, Adobe Flash CS4, Adobe Premier CS4.

-10-   Several related to the subject.

4.8.2.3. MATERIAL RESOURCES

Table.No.2 Material Resources

MATERIALS	QUANTITY
Stationery	6,000 sheets
DvD's	10
CD's	10
Black ink cartridges	1
Color ink cartridges	1
Office supplies	Various
Internet usage	800 hours
Bibliography	books(2)

4.8.2.4. HUMAN RESOURCES

Table.No.3 Human Resources

Human Resources	QUANTITY
Student	1
Advisors	1
Administrators Network 11 B.C.B. GALÁPAGOS	2

4.8.3. ECONOMIC FEASIBILITY

The realization of a project of this type does not require an excessive investment by the proponent, this because the resources are fully available in the 11 B.C.B. GALÁPAGOS, the investment being made is justified by the profit that will be generated by omitting the purchase of licenses to Microsoft due to the use of free software under Linux.

Table.No.4 Costs

RESOURCE	QUANTITY	V. UNIT	SUBTOTAL
Equipment to be used	*	*	*
Internet usage	800 hours	0,20	160.00
Stationery	6000 sheets	0.015	90.00
Network cards	2	50.00	100.00
Cd's	10	0.70	7.00
DvD's	10	1.00	10.00
Black ink cartridges	2	36.00	72.00
Color ink cartridges	1	40.00	40.00
Memories 1gb	2	100	200.00
Hard Disk 1 tera	2	700	1400.00
Bibliography	2	(Avg.)100.00	200.00
Contingencies and Others	10%		227.90
ESTIMATED TOTAL:		USD	2506,90

*The equipment used belongs to the 11BCB GALÁPAGOS and has been detailed in Hardware pp 68.

4.9. EVALUATION

Excellent results were obtained according to the tests performed, both in operation and security, reducing the possibility of internal and external computer attacks by approximately 85%. The LDAP with reliable Open Source for Windows and Linux gave a definitive solution to the problems of secure login between users of different processes. It is recommended to perform this type of study in other corporate networks, especially in the public area where there are no security policies that make them vulnerable to all types of attacks, damage and theft of information via computer. LDAP authentication facilitates and allows maintaining a centralized user administration process. The conformation of the technological platform to support the evaluation process in terms of the installation of servers and free software compared to the use of licensed software servers, the open source is more profitable, secure, fast, optimal and with constant improvements in the implementation mechanisms of LDAP technology. The criteria that are proposed have been gathered from different sources that you can consult in the references section and from the experience of LDAP administrators. A graphical GQ tool will be used to assist the administrator in the performance of each of the proposed security criteria and the default SUSE yast.

BIBLIOGRAPHY .

Bibliography on Operating Systems and Related Technologies:

-1-   Yeong W.,Howes T., and Kille S., "X.500 Free Directory Access Protocol", RFC 1487, July 1993.

-2-   Yeong W., Howes T., and Kille S., "Free Directory Access Protocol," RFC 1777, March 1995.

-3-   Wahl M., Howes T., and Kille S., "Free Directory Access Protocol (v3)", RFC 2251, December 1997.

-4- Wahl M., Coulbeck A., Howes T., and Kille S., "Lightweight Directory Access Protocol (v3): Attribute Syntax Definitions", RFC 2252, December 1997.

-5-   Wahl M.,Kille S., and Howes T., "Free Directory Access Protocol (v3): UTF-8 String Representation of Distinguished Names", RFC 2253, December 1997.

-6-   Howes T., "The String Representation of LDAP Search Filters", RFC 2254, December 1997.

-7-   Howes T., and M. Smith, "The LDAP URL Format", RFC 2255, December 1997.

-8-   Wahl M., "A Summary of the X.500(96) User Schema for use with LDAPv3", RFC 2256, December 1997.

-9-   Howes T., and Smith M., "The LDAP Application Program Interface", RFC 1823, August 1995.

-10-   SCHENKT. Hat Linux Network Administration. Translated from English by Vuelapluma First ed. Spain, Prentice Hall. 2001.

-11-   MAXWELL STEVE, Red Hat Linux Tools for Network Administration. Translated from English by Gustavo Fonseca, Technical Review Jamir Ávila, First Ed. Bogotá, Mac Graw Hill, 2001.

-12-   LAURI B., LAURI P., Apache Definitive Guide, second edition, USA, O' Reily & Associeties Inc 1999.

Bibliography on Operating Systems and Related Technologies

-13-   DOBSON RICK, "Complete Guide to VRML and Applications", McGraw-Hill, 2002.

-14-   WIDWELL, D. SNELL, J and KULCHENKO P. Programming Web Services with SOAP. First Ed. United States, O' Reily & Associates Inc 2001.

INTERNET

-15-   Analysis of network traffic captures. TCP segment interpretation

http://seguridadyredes.nireblog.com/post/2008/01/29/analisis-capturas-trafico-de-red-interpretacion-segmento-tcp-ii-establecimento-conexian-tcp

(2011-01-23)

-16-   Captive Portal Configuration

http://doc.pfsense.org/index.php/Captive Portal

(2011-02-10)

-17-   Administration with open source software

http://www.slideshare.net/miltonvf/administracion-de-redes-y-seguridad-con-software-libre

(2011-02-27)

-18-   LDAP configuration

http://www.turegano.net

(2011-03-17)

-19-   Open LDAP

http://www.openldap.org

(2011-04-04)

-20-   TCP/IP protocol family

http://es.wikipedia.org/wiki/Familia of Internet protocols

(2011-05-03)

-21-   LDAP Administrator's Guide

http://www.openldap.org/doc/admin22/

(2011-06-20)

-22- Communications

http://www.coit.es/

(2011/07/10)

-23- Multiwan

http://sites.google.eom/a/terminuspro.com/internet/manuales/multiwan

(2011-08-04)

-24- RFC791 - Internet Protocol

http://www.faqs.org/rfcs/rfc791.html

(2011-09-15)

-25- RFC793 - Transmission Control Protocol

http://www.faqs.org/rfcs/rfc793.html

(2011-09-19)

-26- RFC1180 - TCP/IP tutorial

http://www.rfc-es.org/rfc/rfc1180-es.txt

(2011-09-21)

-27- Spanish LDAP Manual

http://www.ldap-es.org/node/20

(2011-10-4)

-28- Suse Linux

http://www.suse.com/

(2011-10-8)

-29- LDAP Definitions

http://www.yolinux.com/TUTORIALS/LinuxTutorialLDAP.html

(2011-10- 12)

-30- OPEN LDAP

http://www.redbooks.ibm.com/redbooks/pdfs/sg246193.pdf

(2011-10-15)

-31- FREE RANGE http://www.alcancelibre.org/

(2011-10-22)

-32- GQ PROJECT

http://www. gq-proj ect.org/

(2011-10-28)

-33- LDAP Administration http://ldapadmin.sourceforge.net/

(2011-11-01)

ANNEX 1

The following documents describe how to implement the procedures of the entire LDAP protocol infrastructure in the establishment of a domain with free software under Linux.

CONFIGURATION OF THE LDAP PROTOCOL IN THE ESTABLISHMENT OF A DOMAIN WITH FREE SOFTWARE UNDER LINUX(SUSE) RELIABLE FOR WINDOWS AND LINUX .

-1- The installation is initialized : Select Installation or Installation

Figure.N°18 SUSE LINUX Installation

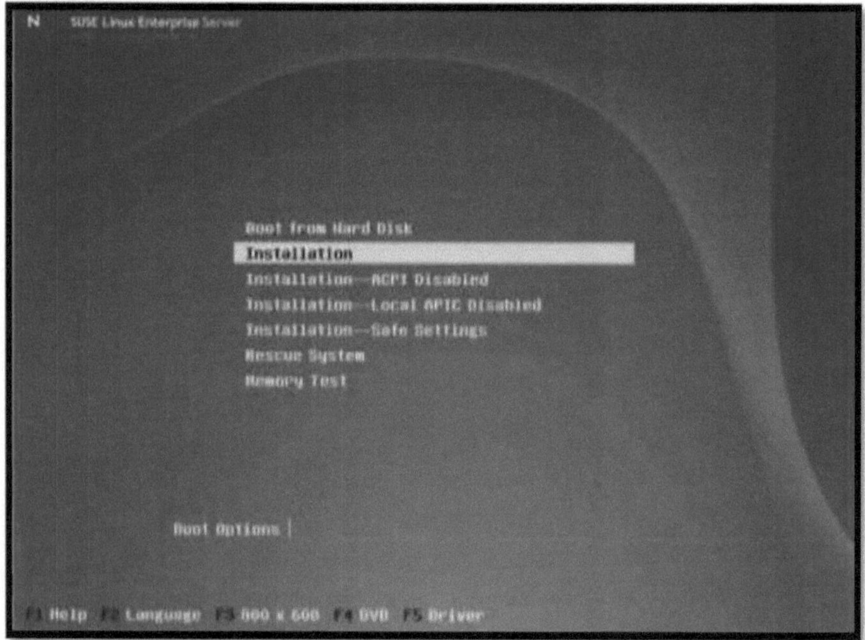

Source: SUSE Linux Operating System Installation

-I- Select the language: English, click on next.

Figure.N°19 Language

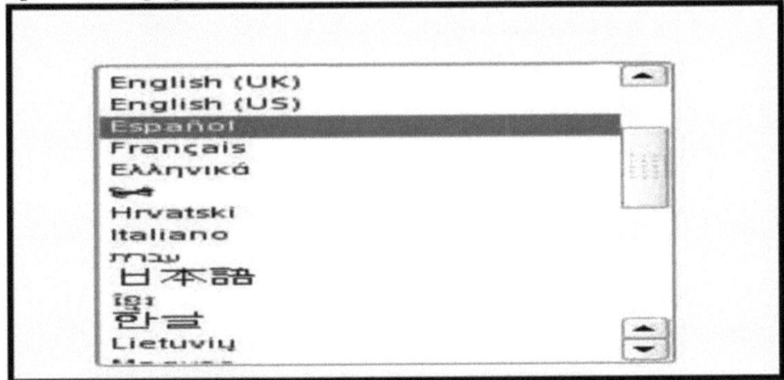

Source: SUSE Linux Operating System Installation

-I- Accept the Linux Suse Enterprise license agreement: Select: If I accept the license agreement, click on the following option:

Figure N° 20 License Agreement

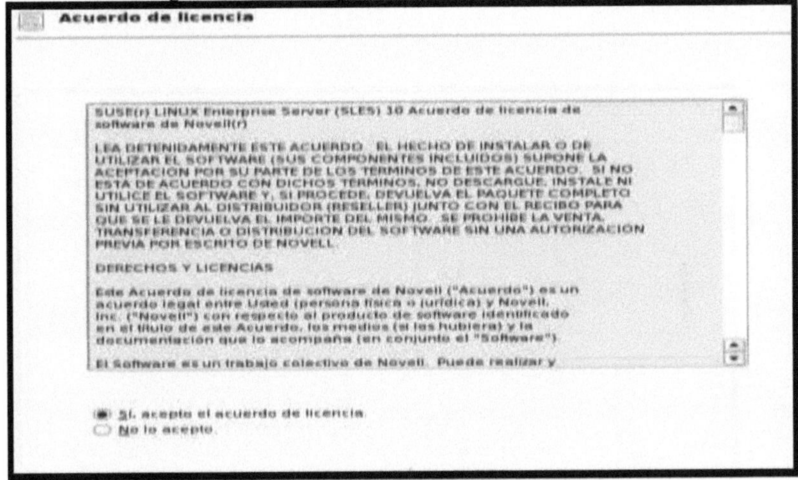

Source: SUSE Linux Operating System Installation

-I- In installation mode: Default New Installation, click next.

Figure N° 21 New SUSE Linux Installation

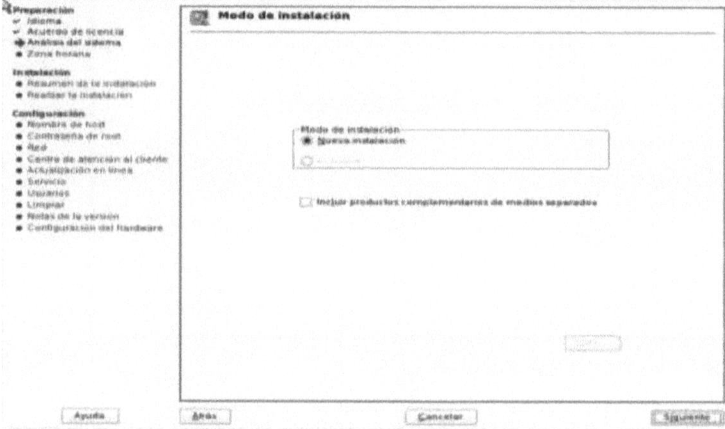

Source: SUSE Linux Operating System Installation

-I- Select the time zone and set the clock time.

Figure. N° 22 Clock and Time Zone

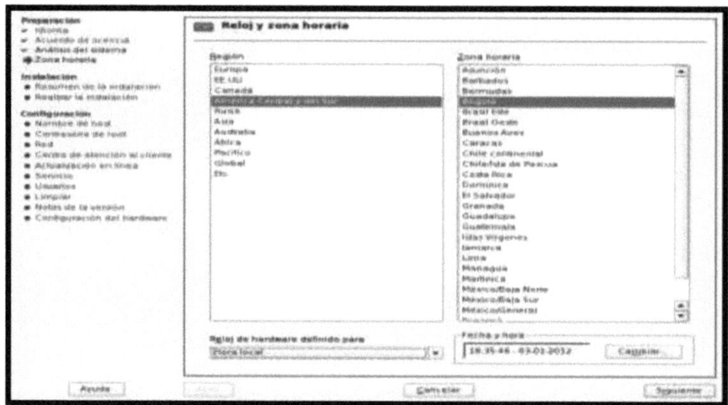

Source: SUSE Linux Operating System

-I- The installation window appears and all the configurations already made, including the LDAP
Directory Service, are set by default, then click on accept.

Figure N° 23 Installation Configuration

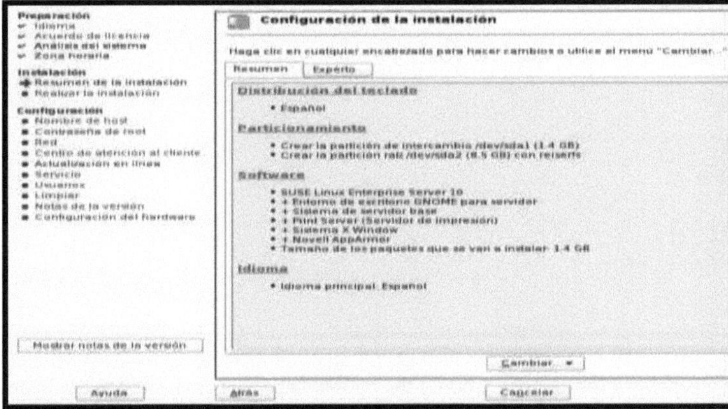

Source: SUSE Linux Operating System

-I- Then start the installation of the respective packages

Figure.N°24 Installation of Packages

Source: SUSE Linux Operating System

-1- Enter the Host name: Server Linux and the domain : brigadagalapagos.mil.ee

Figure N° 25 Host and Domain Name

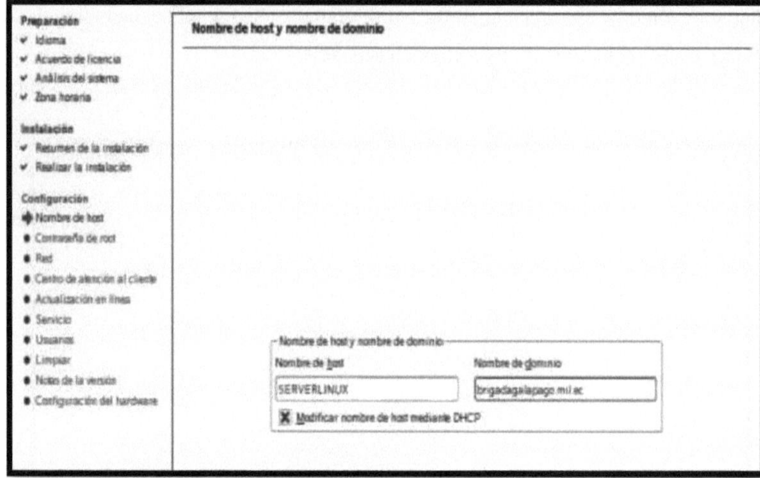

Source: SUSE Linux Operating System

-2- Enter a password for the root. Choose the option that is not connected to the Internet.

Figure. N° 26 Internet Connection Test

Source: SUSE Linux Operating System

-3- Activate the LDAP server and click next.

Figure.N°27 LDAP Server Configuration

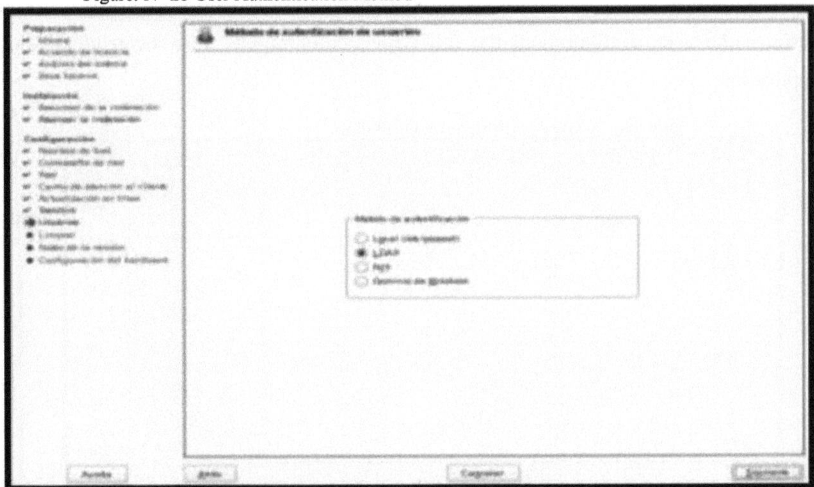

Source: SUSE Linux Operating System

-I- The method of user authentication

Figure. N° 28 User Authentication Method

Source: SUSE Linux Operating System

-4- User authentication and LDAP client and LDAP server address 127.0.0.1

Figure .N° 29 LDAP Client Configuration

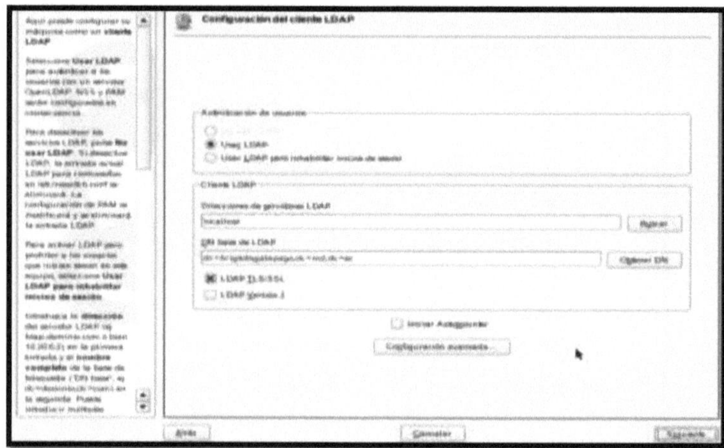

Source: SUSE Linux Operating System

-1- Create a LDAP user, as user name take the first letter of the first name and the full last name together and the password will be <u>Riobamba.</u>

-2- Finalize the hardware configuration.

-3- Enter and download the GQ file; then double click and proceed to run the GQ. In order to perform the user configuration, the following configurations must be made in the GQ application.

Figure. No. 30 GQ Application Administration

Source: SUSE Linux Operating System (gq)

-4- As you can see this dc=brigadagalapagos,dc=mil,dc=ec, then open and we get the hierarchical structure of users

Figure N° 31 User Accounts gq

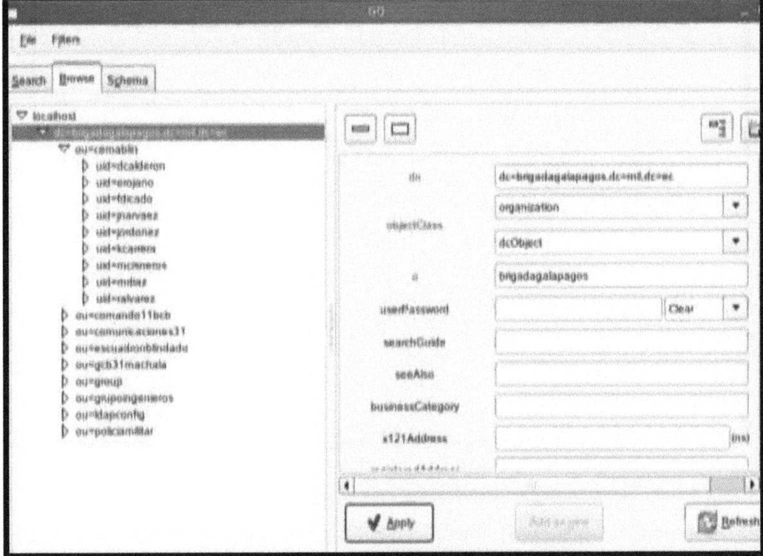

Source: SUSE Linux Operating System (gq)

-5- Attributes and inputs are randomly set for optimal GQ configuration.

Figure.N°32 User Management

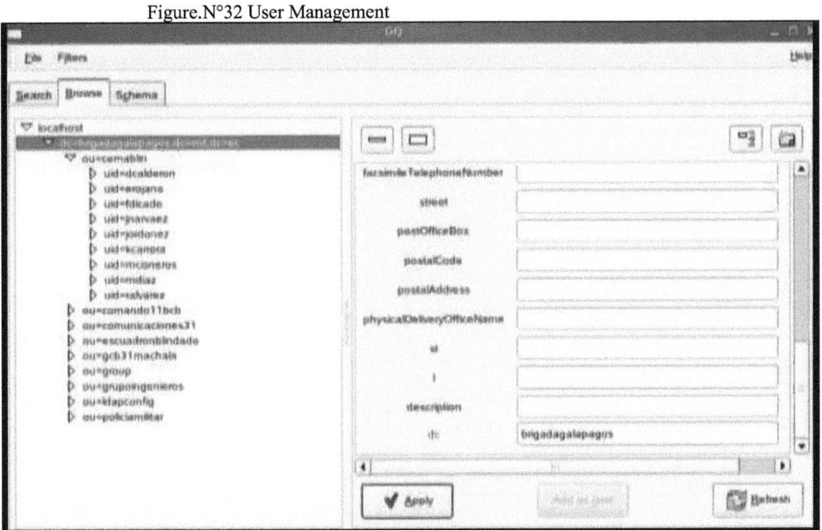

Source: SUSE Linux Operating System (gq)

-I- Configure each unit as follows: ou=cemablin, dc=brigadagalapagos, dc=mil, dc=ec

Figure N° 33Characteristics of each entry and attribute

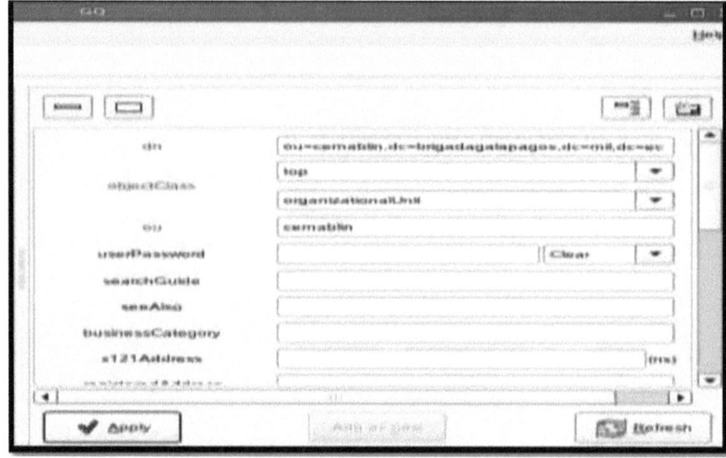

Source: SUSE Linux Operating System (gq)

-6- Each attribute is set as shown in the image below:

Figure N° 34 Objects

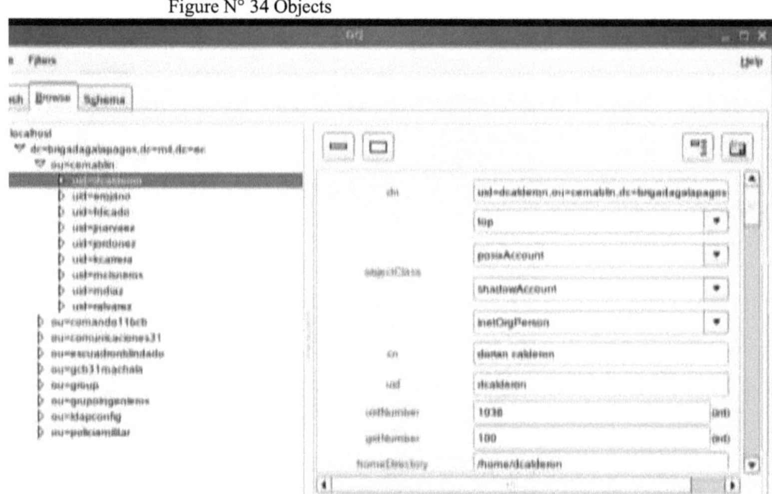

-1- As previously observed, the users of each PC would be configured as follows: uid=dcalderon,ou=cemablin,dc=brigadagalapagos,dc=mil,dc=ec, and the corresponding attributes are written for a stable configuration.

Figure. N° 35 Encrypted Key

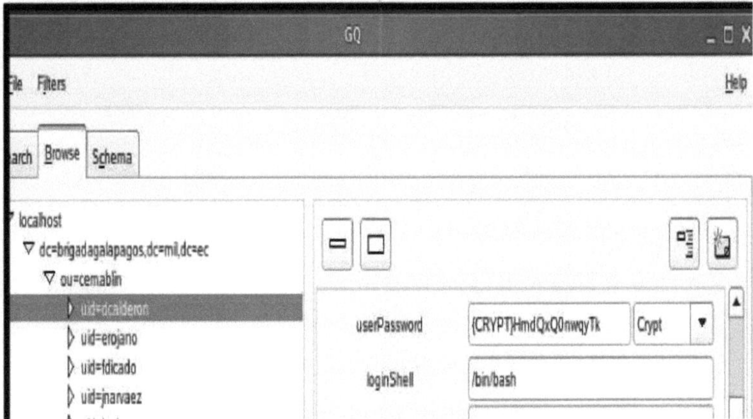

Source: SUSE Linux Operating System (gq)

-2- Continue filling in the attributes

Figure N° 36 Personal User UID

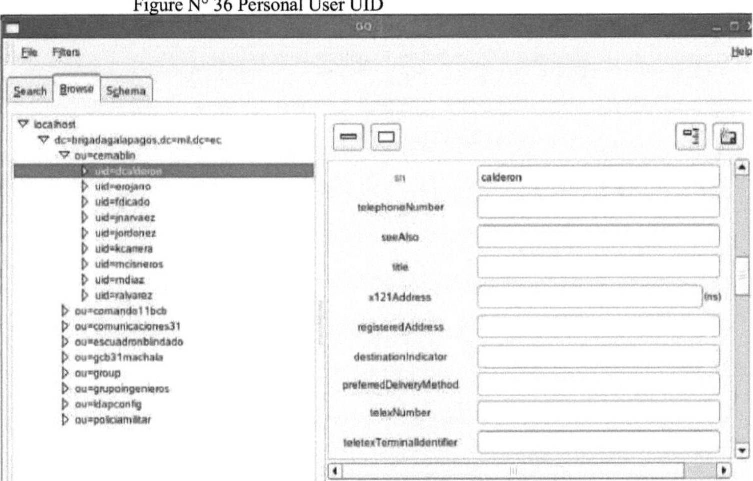

Source: SUSE Linux Operating System (gq)

-4- We proceed to configure the YAST (network card) part.

Figure.N°37Yast Administration (network cards)

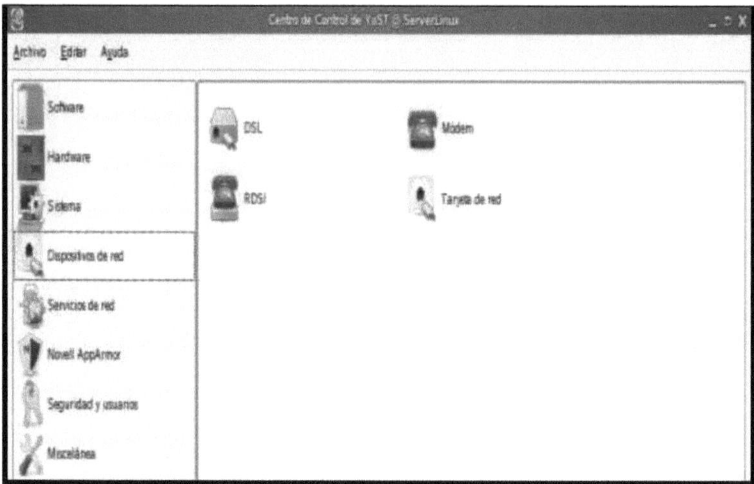

Source: SUSE Linux Operating System(yast)

-5- Continue with the network configuration method

Figure N° 38 Network configuration method

Source: SUSE Linux Operating System (yast)
Figure.N°39 Summary configuration of network cards
Source: SUSE Linux Operating System (yast)
-I- Click on the edit option

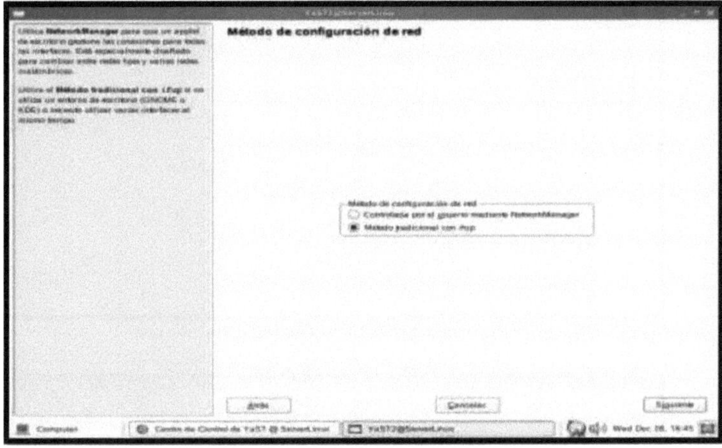

Figure.N°40 Configuration of the network address

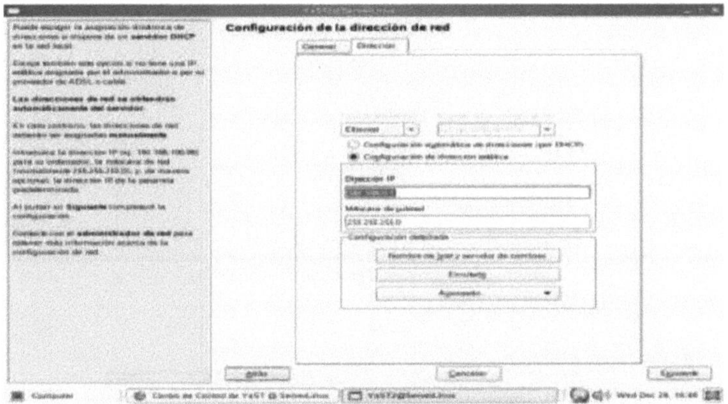

Source: SUSE Linux Operating System (yast)

-I- DHCP Configuration: In global configuration of the DHCP server, the
domain name was changed from brigadagalapagos.mil.ec to brigadagalapago because samba does
not support more than 15 characters but this does not affect the LDAP Server configuration.

Figure.No.41DHCP, Global Adjustments

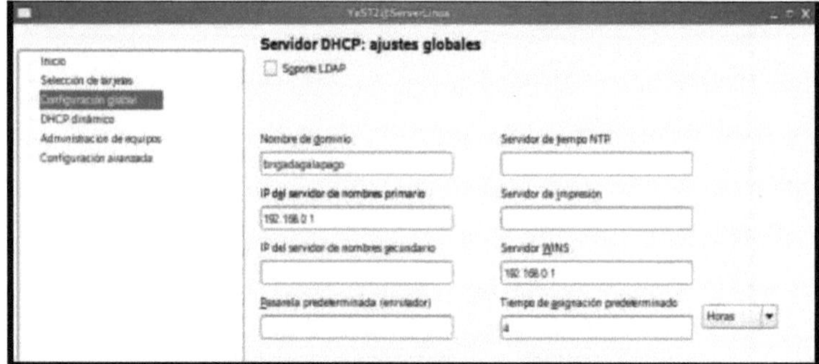

Source: SUSE Linux Operating System (yast)

Figure .No. 42 Dynamic DHCP Server

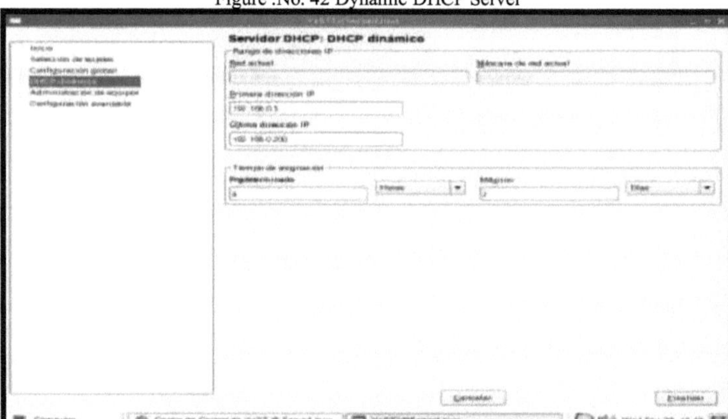

Source: SUSE Linux Operating System (yast)

-I- SAMBA Server Configuration

Figure.N°43 Samba Configuration, Identity

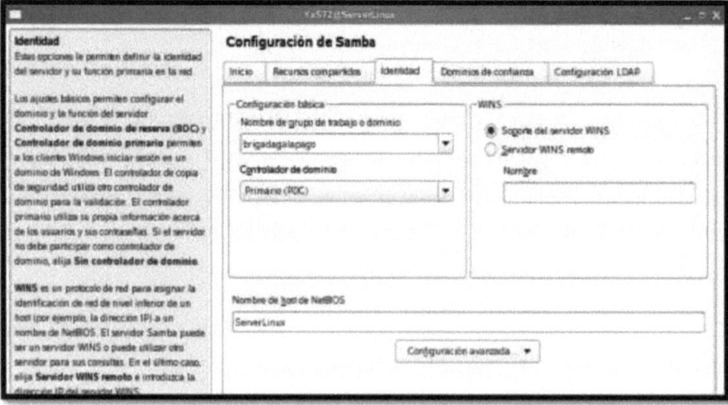

Source: SUSE Linux Operating System (yast)

Figure. N° 44 Samba, LDAP configuration

Source: SUSE Linux Operating System (yast)

-I- Creation of a Common certificate for the Servers: Click on Certification Authorities Management.

Figure. N° 45

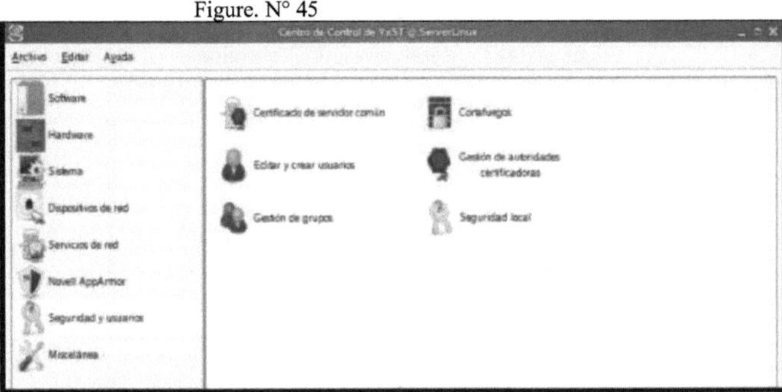

Source: SUSE Linux Operating System (yast)

-I- Create a Root CA

Figure.N°46 Root Certification Authority

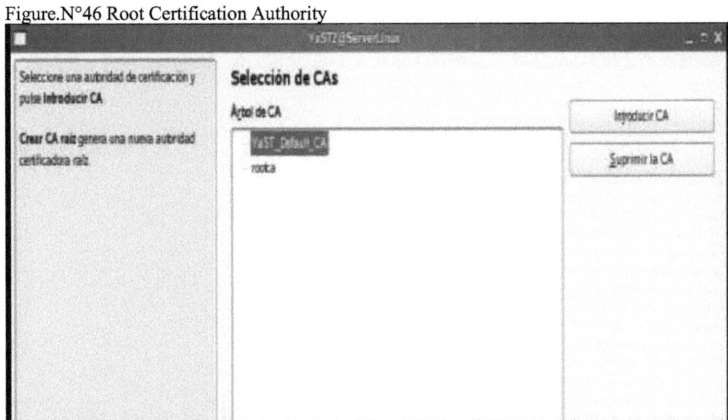

Source: SUSE Linux Operating System (yast)

-I- Create a New Root CA

Figure N° 47 New Root

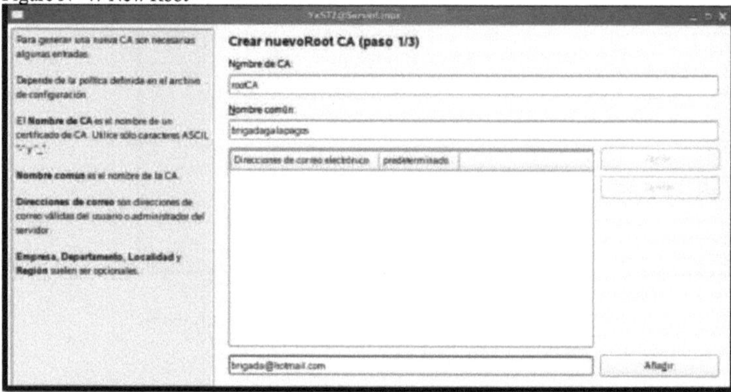

Source: SUSE Linux Operating System (yast)

Figure.N°48 Certificate Authority Validation

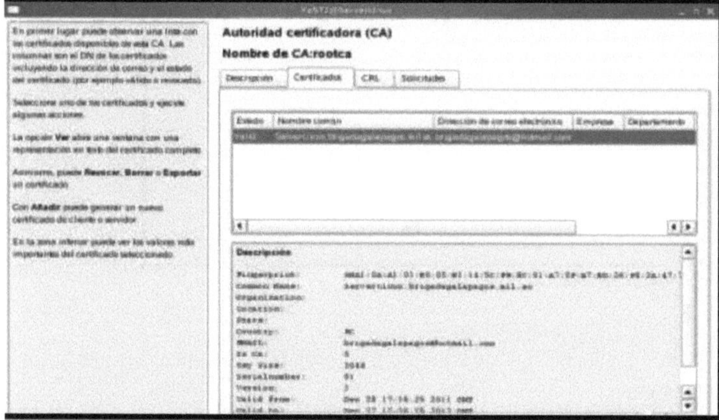

Source: SUSE Linux Operating System (yast)

Figure N° 49 LDAP configuration in yast

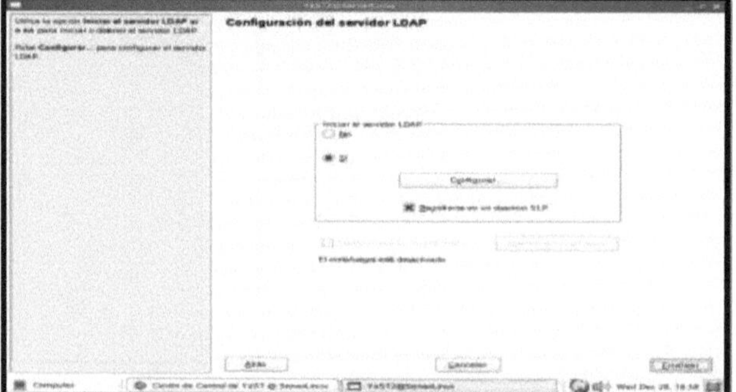

Source: SUSE Linux Operating System (yast)

-I- Click on the configure option

-1- In the TLS option activate the option Yes.

Figure.N°50 Global Configuration

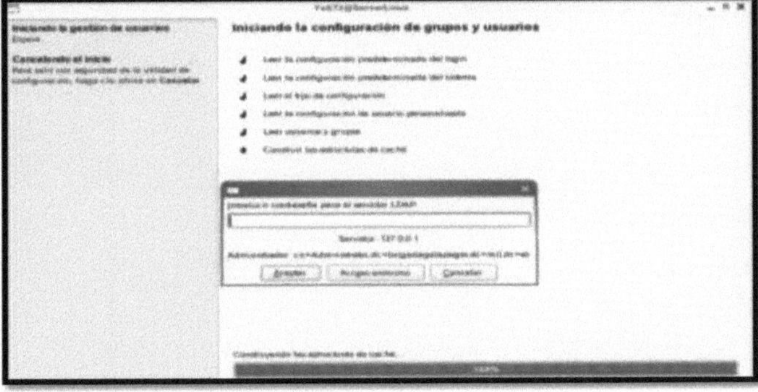

Source: SUSE Linux Operating System (yast)

-2- Click on select Certificate and then select the common certificate to be created.

-3- The ldap users must be added after having configured the servers by adding them to the ntusers group for Windows and antGuests for Linux. ....

Figure.N°51Configuration of the network address

Source: SUSE Linux Operating System (yast)

-4- Start editing groups and users in yast and you can edit, create, delete,

users according to the requirements of the 11BCB GALÁPAGOS.

-I- LDAP User Creation

Figure N° 53 LDAP user

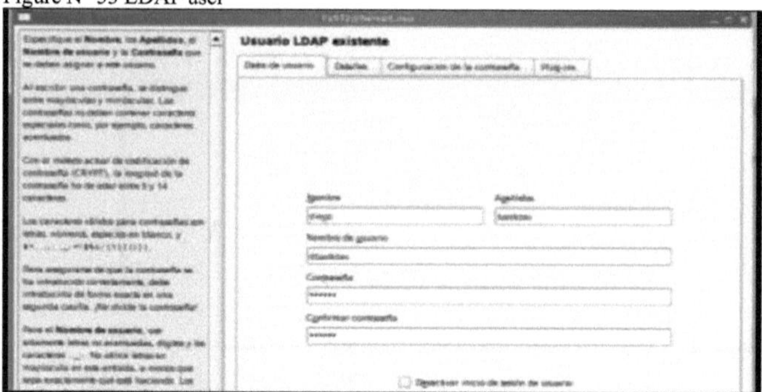

Source: Yast User Configuration in SUSE

The structure of our directory tree is added. An LDIF file is created with the following content:

dn: ou=es,dc=setec,dc=com

ou: es

description: Sede en España

objectclass: organizationalunit

dn: ou=pt,dc=setec,dc=com

ou: pt

description: Sede en Portugal

objectclass: organizationalunit

dn: ou=us,dc=setec,dc=com

ou: us

description: Sede en USA

objectclass: organizationalunit

dn: ou=mad,ou=es,dc=setec,dc=com

ou: mad

description: Sede en Madrid (Spain)

objectclass: organizationalunit

dn: ou=bcn,ou=es,dc=setec,dc=com

ou: bcn

description: Sede en Barcelona (Spain)

objectclass: organizationalunit

dn: ou=lis,ou=pt,dc=setec,dc=com

ou: lis

description: Sede en Lisboa (Portugal)

objectclass: organizationalunit

dn: ou=ny,ou=us,dc=setec,dc=com

ou: ny

description: Sede en New York (USA)

objectclass: organizationalunit

dn: ou=sfo,ou=us,dc=setec,dc=com

ou: sfo

description: Sede en San Francisco (USA)

objectclass: organizationalunit

dn: ou=bos,ou=us,dc=setec,dc=com

ou: bos

description: Sede en Boston (USA)

objectclass: organizationalunit

Se lo salva como ldif2.ldif y se lo carga en el servidor LDAP con el siguiente comando:

ldapadd -x -D "cn=root,dc=setec,dc=com" -W -f ldif2.ldif

and check that the operation has been performed correctly with the command:

ldapsearch -x -b 'dc=setec,dc=com' '(objectclass=*)'

-I- First entries

Once the whole directory structure has been created, the first users will be introduced. For this purpose, an LDIF file with the contents is created again:

dn: uid=jmsuarez,ou=mad,ou=es,dc=setec,dc=com

uid: jmsuarez

cn: Jose Manuel

sn: Manuel

objectclass: top

objectclass: person

objectclass: posixaccount

loginshell: /bin/bash

uidnumber: 99

gidnumber: 99

homedirectory: /home/jmsuarez

userpassword: secret1

 dn: uid=msilva,ou=lis,ou=pt,dc=setec,dc=com

uid: msilva

cn: Mauro

sn: Silva

objectclass: top

objectclass: person

objectclass: posixaccount

loginshell: /bin/bash

uidnumber: 100

gidnumber: 100

homedirectory: /home/msilva

userpassword: secret2

dn: uid=jsmith,ou=ny,ou=us,dc=setec,dc=com

uid: jsmith

cn: John

sn: Smith

objectclass: top

objectclass: person

objectclass: posixaccount

loginshell: /bin/bash

uidnumber: 102

gidnumber: 102

homedirectory: /home/jsmith

userpassword: secret3

Se lo salva como ldif3.ldif y se lo carga en el servidor LDAP con el siguiente comando:

ldapadd -x -D "cn=root,dc=setec,dc=com" -W -f ldif3.ldif

- -I- The operation can be checked with the commands:

ldapsearch -x -b 'dc=setec,dc=com' uid=jmsuarez

ldapsearch -x -b 'dc=setec,dc=com' uid=msilva

ldapsearch -x -b 'dc=setec,dc=com' uid=jsmith

- -I- The following commands are used to search, this search will display all directory entries starting from the branch "dc=setec,dc=com".

ldapsearch -x -b 'dc=setec,dc=com' '(objectclass=*)'

Con esta búsqueda se obtiene los datos del usuario jmsuarez

ldapsearch -x -b 'dc=setec,dc=com' uid=jmsuarez

Con esta otra se busca al usuario jmsuarez en la rama

"ou=mad,ou=es,dc=setec,dc=com"

 ldapsearch -x -b 'ou=mad,ou=es,dc=setec,dc=com' uid=jmsuarez

Con esta otra en la rama "ou=us,dc=setec,dc=com" (no mostrará ningún resultado)

ldapsearch -x -b 'ou=us,dc=setec,dc=com' uid=jmsuarez

- -I- Modification of attributes

If you wish to modify an attribute of an entry, you can do so by creating an LDIF file and using the ldapmodify command.

For example, if you want to change the last name (sn) to the entry "uid=jmsuarez", an LDIF file (ldif4.ldif) with the following content is created:

dn:uid=jmsuarez,ou=mad,ou=es,dc=setec,dc=com

changetype:modify

replace: sn

sn: San Martin

And then the following command is executed

ldapmodify -x -D "cn=root,dc=setec,dc=com" -W -f ldif4.ldif

Se puede comprobar la operación con el comando:

ldapsearch -x -b 'dc=setec,dc=com' uid=jmsuarez

-I- Attribute deletion

If you want to delete an attribute from an entry, you do it by creating an LDIF file and using the ldapmodify command. For example, to delete the attribute last name (sn) from the entry "uid=jmsuarez", an LDIF file (ldif4.ldif) with the following content is created:

dn:uid=jmsuarez,ou=mad,ou=es,dc=setec,dc=com

changetype:delete

delete: sn

And then the command is executed:

ldapmodify -x -D "cn=root,dc=setec,dc=com" -W -f ldif4.ldif

By being able to check the operation with the command:

    ldapsearch -x -b 'dc=setec,dc=com' uid=jmsuarez

ANNEX 2

PROJECT CHARTER

Main information and project authorization	
Date: March 28, 2011	**Name of the project:** Implementation of the LDAP protocol in the establishment of a domain with free software under Linux in the BRIGADA DE CABALLERÍA BLINDADA No.11 "GALÁPAGOS" (Armored Cavalry Brigade No.11 "GALÁPAGOS").
Areas of knowledge: NETWORKS OF COMPUTERS, SOFTWARE, LINUX.	**Area of application:** Sector Institution Public
Start date of the Feasible Project: March 28, 2011	**Tentative date of completion of the feasible project**: March 28, 2012
Project Objectives: Implement an LDAP directory system in the BRIGADA DE CABALLERÍA BLINDADA No.11 "GALÁPAGOS", so that each user has a directory associated with individual authentication.	
Specific objectives: 4- Install, configure and start up an LDAP directory server. 4- Populate the directories of such a server with the information of each user. 4- To provide security to users against the Look Over the Shoulder attack. 4- To provoke in the current administrators a re-analysis of the security of the service.	
Need for the Project : The problem lies in the lack of authentication of the users of the military personnel and public servants working in the BRIGADA DE CABALLERÍA BLINDADA No.11 "GALÁPAGOS" (Armored Cavalry Brigade No.11 "GALÁPAGOS"), since unauthorized access to information would cause an unauthorized access to the information. The unauthorized access to the information would cause a institutional imbalance, for which the implementation of the LDAP authentication protocol has been considered.	

Due to the lack of knowledge of Linux, military and public service personnel have not previously implemented a security authentication protocol such as LDAP in the institution, being a priority need for the BRIGADE to solve this problem immediately.

Impact justification :

This work is particularly limited to the BRIGADA DE CABALLERÍA BLINDADA No.11 "GALÁPAGOS", due to the fact that some aspects within the internal networks are specific to each organization, such as technological and organizational infrastructure.

This feasible project presents an analysis and implementation of security over LDAP in the data network of the BRIGADA DE CABALLERÍA BLINDADA No.11 "GALÁPAGOS", and given the impossibility of reviewing each and every one of the existing problems, we have chosen to select a significant set of authentication solution close to the needs of the institution.

According to the research carried out, there is no service equal or similar to the proposal that allows having network services with any security policy that allows access to the directory information through a scheme:

    4- Client - Server.

    4- Define a hierarchical structure of objects or entries in the form of a tree.

    4- Interactivity with the user, authentication, etc.

In addition, this will prevent any type of attack, especially the "look over the shoulder" attack, in a more secure and reliable way. The implementation of these services constitutes a success factor, since they will contribute to achieve the objectives proposed in the institution.

Direct Beneficiaries:

armored cavalry brigade no.11 "galapagos".

Indirect Beneficiaries: General Staff	
Approved by :	**Signature :**

ANNEX 3

PROPOSED DRAFT:

LDAP PROTOCOL IMPLEMENTATION IN THE ESTABLISHMENT OF AN DOMAIN WITH FREE SOFTWARE UNDER LINUX IN THE BRIGADE OF ARMORED CABALRY No. 11 GALÁPAGOS

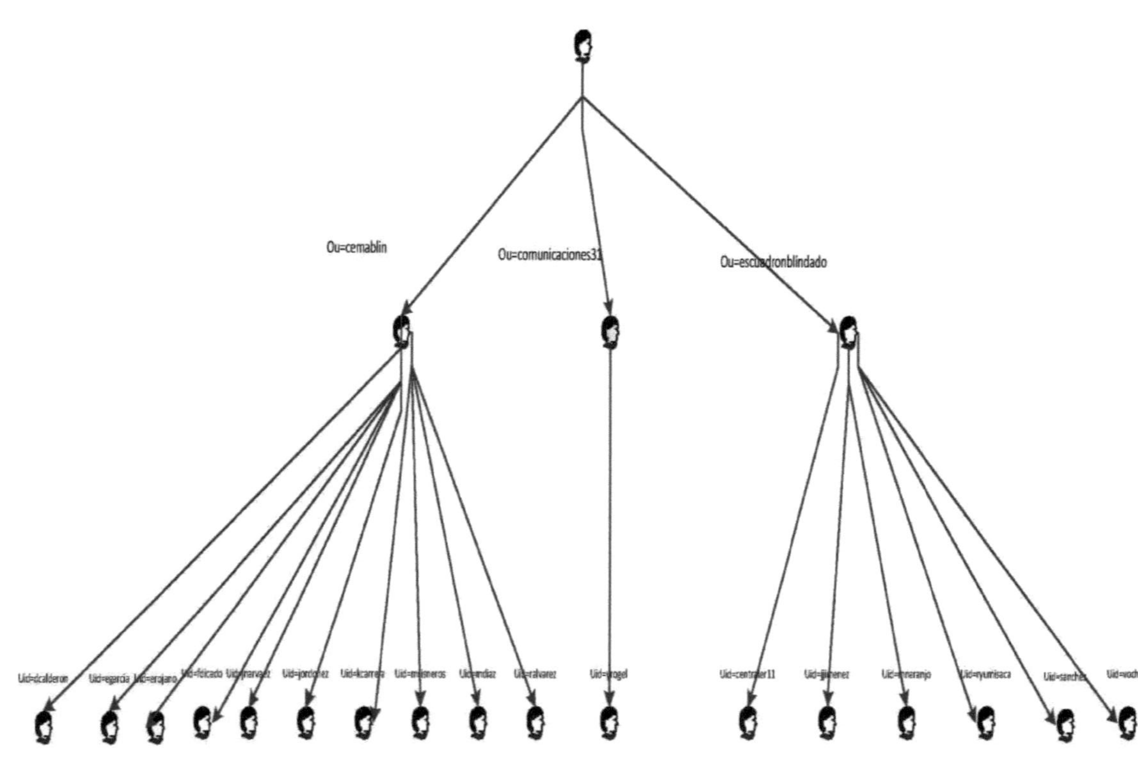

Dc=brigadagalapagos,dc=mil,dc=ec
Ou=cemablin
Ou=comunicaciones31
Ou=escuadronblindado
Uid=dcalderon
Uid=egarcia
Uid=erojano
Uid=fdicado
Uid=narvaez
Uid=jordonez
Uid=kcarrera
Uid=mesneros
Uid=ndiaz
Uid=ralvarez
Uid=rogel
Uid=centraler11
Uid=jjimenez
Uid=mnaranjo
Uid=ryumisaca
Uid=sanchez
Uid=vochoa

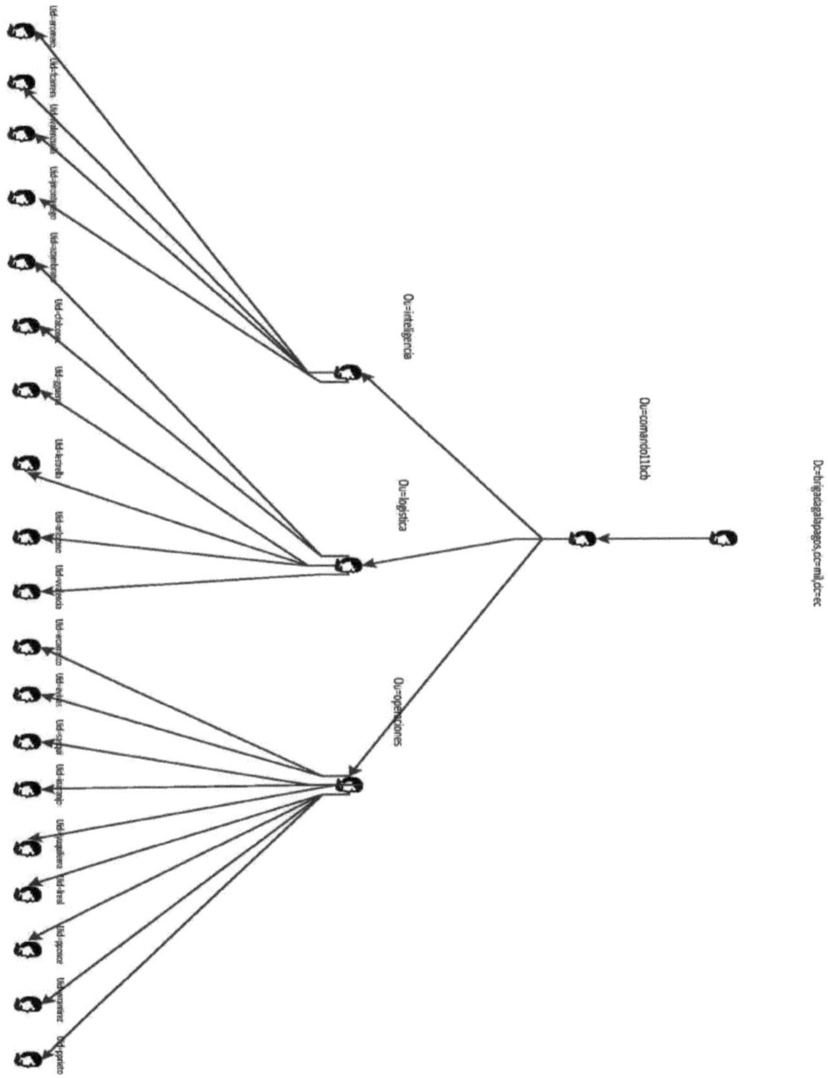
Dc=brigadagalapagos,dc=mil,dc=ec
Ou=comando11bcb
Ou=inteligencia
Ou=logistica
Ou=operaciones

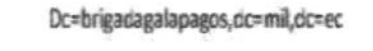

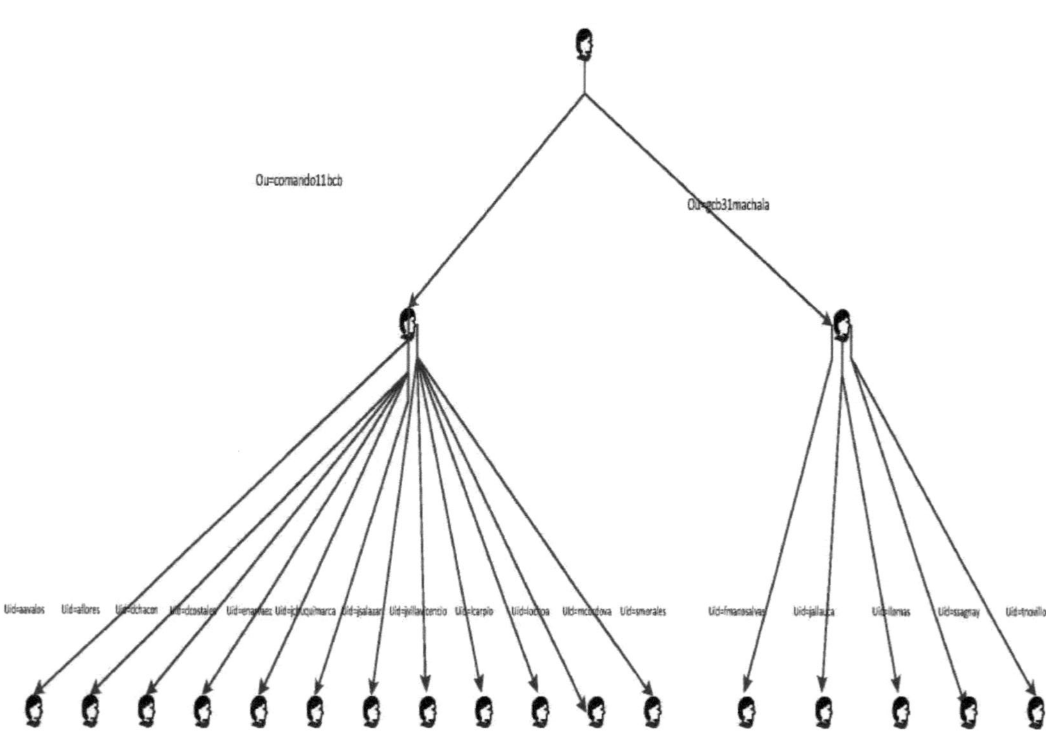

Dc=brigadagalapagos,dc=mil,dc=ec
Ou=comando11bcb
Ou=gcb31machala
Uid=aavalos
Uid=aflores
Uid=cchacon
Uid=ccostales
Uid=enarvaez
Uid=jchuquimarca
Uid=jsalazar
Uid=jvillavicencio
Uid=lcarpio
Uid=lochoa
Uid=mcordova
Uid=smorales
Uid=fmanosalvas
Uid=jallauca
Uid=llamas
Uid=ssagnay
Uid=trosillo

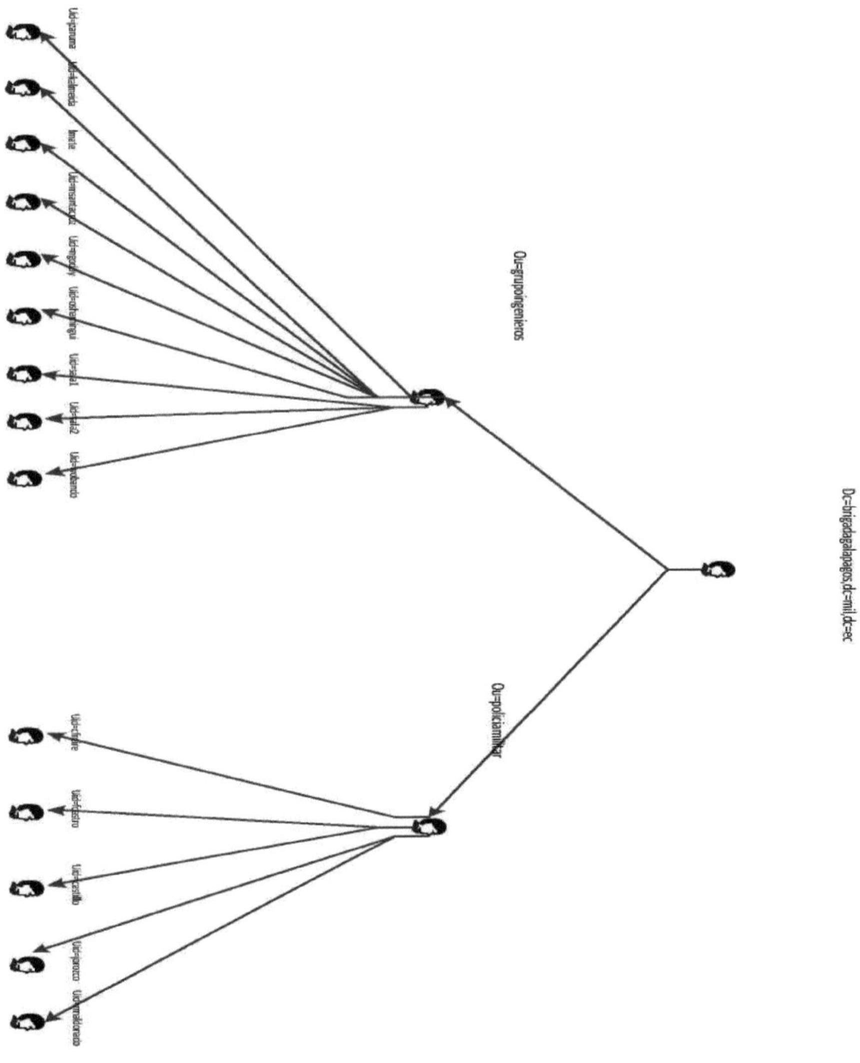

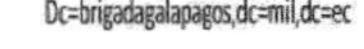
Dc=brigadagalapagos,dc=mil,dc=ec
Ou=grupoingenieros
Ou=policiamilitar
Uid=jcaruma
Uid=kalmeida
lmate
Uid=msantacruz
Uid=ngoday
Uid=oshemingui
Uid=sala1
Uid=sala2
Uid=probando
Uid=cfreire
Uid=fcastro
Uid=castillo
Uid=jorozco
Uid=amaldonado